P9-CFV-367

VOLLEYBALL

BY VICTORIA SHERROW

Lucent Books, Inc.
San Diego, California

Titles in The History of Sports Series include:
- Baseball
- Basketball
- Football
- Golf
- Hockey
- Soccer
- Track and Field
- Wrestling
- Volleyball

Library of Congress Cataloging-in-Publication Data

NC RM BK SD

Sherrow, Victoria.
Volleyball / by Victoria Sherrow.
p. cm. — (History of sports)
Includes bibliographical references (p.) and index.
Summary: Discusses the history and evolution of the game of volleyball, its recent popularity, and famous personalities in the game's history.
ISBN 1-56006-961-9 (hbk. : alk. paper)
1. Volleyball—History—Juvenile literature. [1. Volleyball—History.] I. Title. II. Series.
GV1015.34 .S54 2002
796.325—dc21

2001004233

10911 Technology Place, San Diego, CA 92127
Printed in the U.S.A.

Contents

Foreword

More than many areas of human endeavor, sports give us the opportunity to see the possibilities in our physical selves. As participants, we all too quickly find limits to how fast we can run, how high we can jump, how far and straight we can hit a golf ball. But as spectators we can surpass those limits as we view the accomplishments of others and see how fast, how smooth, and how strong a human being can be. We marvel at the gravity-defying leaps of a Michael Jordan as he strains towards a basketball hoop or at the dribbling of a Mia Hamm as she eludes defenders on the soccer field. We shake our heads in disbelief at the talents of a young Tiger Woods hitting an approach shot to the green or the speed of a Carl Lewis as he appears to glide around an Olympic track.

These are what the sports media call "the oohs and ahhs" of sports—the stuff of highlight reels and *Sports Illustrated* covers. But to understand a sport only in the context of its most artistic modern athletes is shortsighted, for it does little justice to the accomplishments of the athletes *or* to the sport itself. Far more wise is to view a sport as a continuum—a constantly moving, evolving process. On this continuum are not only the superstars of today, but the people who first played the sport, who thought about rules and strategies that would make it more challenging to play as well as a delight to watch.

Lucent Books' series, *The History of Sports,* provides such a continuum. Each book explores the development of a sport from its basic roots onward, and tries to answer questions that a reader might wonder about. Who were its first players, and what sorts of rules did the sport have then? What kinds of equipment were used in the beginning and what changes have taken place over the years?

Each title in *The History of Sports* also identifies key individuals in the sport's history—people whose leadership or skills have made a difference in the way the sport is played today. Included will be the easily recognized names, the Mia Hamms and the Sammy Sosas, the Wilt Chamberlains and the Wilma Rudolphs. But there are also the names of past greats, people like baseball's King Kelly, soccer's Sir Stanley Matthews, and basketball's Hank Luisetti—who may be less familiar today, but were as synonymous with their sports at one time as the "oohs and ahhs" players of today.

Finally, the series looks at the aspects of a sport that are particularly important in its current point on the continuum. Baseball today is better understood knowing about salary caps and union negotiators. One cannot truly know modern soccer without knowing about the specter of fan violence at matches. And learning about the role of instant replay is critical to a thorough understanding of today's professional football games. In viewing a sport as a continuum, the strides that have been made along the way are that much more admirable. It is a richer view, and one that shows how yesterday's limits have been surpassed—and how the limits of today are the possibilities of athletes in the future.

From Recreation to Competition

Although volleyball was originally designed for middle-aged men who were not vigorous enough to play basketball, it has evolved into a fast-paced and highly competitive sport for both men and women. Today's players dive and leap as they work together to keep the ball from hitting the floor on their side and then smash it into their opponent's court. They must think and act quickly and strategically, both in offensive and defensive play. This is "power volleyball," not the relatively tame game that debuted in Massachusetts back in 1895, and it offers excitement for both players and spectators. Fans can see this kind of volleyball at various amateur competitions or in pro tournaments, where players compete each year for millions of dollars in prizes.

However, volleyball can also be purely recreational, played for fun or for exercise. People of all ages enjoy the game in schools, community centers, parks, playgrounds, and beaches. Groups at a picnic, barbecue, or backyard party can simply hit the ball back and forth across the net, leaving the finer points of the game to more advanced players.

Both recreational and competitive volleyball are immensely popular, and globally volleyball ranks second only to soccer as a participation sport. As of 2001, about 46 million Americans played volleyball and some 800 million people from more than a hundred countries around the world played at least once a week for fun or in local, regional, and international competitions. In recent decades

Speed, excitement, and intense competition are the hallmarks of modern volleyball.

volleyball has become the high school and collegiate sport with the highest number of players, and the numbers keep rising each year. As of 2000 more than twelve thousand high schools in the United States had volleyball teams.

Several factors account for this growth in popularity. Volleyball is a versatile game that suits a wide range of players and settings. Teams can be made up of one or both genders, and people can play at different levels. The game has also been adapted for people with disabilities, who play "sitting volleyball" in wheelchairs. Recreational players can build teams around the number of people who want to play. They need not conform to the official rule of six players per side for indoor volleyball or two players per side, the usual number for competitive beach volleyball.

The game is also versatile because it can be played on indoor courts or outdoors, on a hard surface like wood or on a sandy beach, or, in the case of water volleyball, in a pool. Volleyball does not require much equipment—just a ball and a net, or a rope that can serve as a net—and it can be adapted to different situations. Players can change net heights and court dimensions to suit their needs and the people involved. Furthermore, because the ball does not bounce during play, the court need not be perfectly smooth or straight. Court boundaries can be marked off with stones or other objects or with marks in the sand.

There are strict rules for competitive volleyball, however, and teams aim to build skill, strategy, and speed. Height is an advantage for players, and the world's best teams often feature tall players. Many people first play competitive volleyball as students in junior high school, high school, or college, where they can try out for intramural, club, junior varsity, and varsity teams that engage in interscholastic competition. There are also thousands of regional club organizations whose members form teams based on players' levels of skill and commitment. Club volleyball teams may compete locally, regionally, or nationally, and are usually grouped according to age level. International play takes many forms and includes the Summer Olympics, where indoor and beach volleyball are events for men and women.

At each level of play, both individual skills and teamwork are important. A team with devoted players and good chemistry

The fun and versatility of volleyball has made it popular around the world.

possesses two essential ingredients for success. In the relatively small space of a volleyball court, teamwork can make the difference between victory and defeat. Working together and communicating clearly helps a team maximize each play and also to avoid "traffic jams" on the court. Watching this teamwork—whether it is a six-person indoor team or a two-person team on the beach—is part of the drama of a good volleyball match.

Volleyball has a fascinating history. The rules and techniques have changed greatly from its simple beginnings as people around the world have adopted the game and developed national and international organizations. Creativity and dedication have made volleyball into one of the world's top sports, a game that can challenge the most elite players at the Olympics or simply add fun to a family picnic at the beach.

A New Team Sport

Volleyball was created more than a century ago on the heels of basketball, another sport that was destined to become tremendously popular. Both sports emerged in New England during the 1890s as recreational games created by Young Men's Christian Association (YMCA) instructors. Volleyball came about when William G. Morgan found that many of the men who belonged to the YMCA under his direction were not young and strong enough to play basketball well. He then came up with a sport he called "mintonette"—the forerunner of today's volleyball. Little did Morgan realize that the game he designed would spread around the world and become one of the most popular games in history, as well as a highly competitive sport.

Born at the YMCA

The popular team sports of basketball and volleyball both have their roots in Massachusetts. Dr. James Naismith, a Canadian clergyman, was an outstanding athlete himself when he became a physical education instructor at the YMCA in Springfield. In 1891 he began looking for a game that the active young men in his program would enjoy playing indoors when cold or rainy weather prevented them from playing football or baseball. As he discussed various possibilities with his fellow instructors, Naismith said that the game should be "interesting, easy to learn, and easy to play in the winter and by artificial light."[1] Through trial and error, Naismith came up with a game he named "Basket Ball," in which two teams

William G. Morgan invented a new game in 1891 which he named "mintonette," the forerunner of today's volleyball.

competed against each other using a large ball and two peach baskets attached to poles on either side of the court.

Basketball was a big success, both with YMCA members and staff. One of the young instructors who enjoyed playing the game was William G. Morgan, who later became director of physical education at the YMCA in Holyoke, Massachusetts. Soon after he arrived, Morgan enthusiastically introduced the new game of basketball to the men in Holyoke, but the population there included many older businessmen. Although they liked team sports and competition, basketball involved a fair amount of physical contact and the fast pace of the game tired them. Morgan later wrote, "Basket ball seemed quite suited to the younger men, but there was a need for something for the older ones not so rough or severe."[2]

Morgan resolved to come up with another winter sport that would better suit the abilities and fitness levels of these players. As he thought about this new game, he looked at elements from several different sports—basketball, baseball, tennis, and handball—and began to blend them into something that would suit his needs.

Like tennis, Morgan's game was played on a rectangular court with a net across the center, but the players did not need rackets. Morgan decided players could use their hands to bat the ball back and forth, which would reduce the amount of equipment and permit more people to play at one time. He positioned the net between two poles about six feet six inches above the floor, so it would be several inches higher than the average player's head. The court was also small enough so players would not have to run over a large area. There were two teams, as in baseball and basketball. Players stood on either side of the net, which eliminated the physical contact that occurs in basketball. Using their hands, they hit a lightweight rubber ball—actually an inflated basketball bladder—back and forth until it either hit the floor or went outside the court's boundary lines.

Morgan organized his game into innings consisting of three serves by each team. There were nine innings in his game, the same number as in baseball. Teams could hit the ball as many times on their side as they

The Holyoke, Massachusetts, YMCA fostered the game in the early days.

wanted in an effort to get the ball over the net into the opponent's side of the court. If the receiving team did not return the ball before it hit the floor, that meant the other side won a point if they had served or gained control of the serve if they had received.

As Morgan had hoped, his invention was a hit among his older players, and soon younger men also began to play. In the beginning, Morgan called the game "mintonette" because he thought it resembled badminton, a game in which players hit a birdie back and forth over a net with rackets.

"Mintonette" Becomes "Volley Ball"

Delighted that mintonette was so successful, Morgan voluntarily shared it with others. In 1896, about a year after he introduced the game, Morgan presented an exhibition match for a group of YMCA physical education directors attending their annual conference at the YMCA Training School, now Springfield College. One spectator, Dr. Alfred Halsted, suggested that Morgan change the name of the game from "mintonette" to "volley ball," because the players were volleying the ball back and forth with each hit. The first official volleyball game was played at Springfield College on July 7, 1896.

When the exhibition ended, the physical education instructors at the conference asked Morgan to write down the rules of the game. He obligingly wrote them down by hand and passed them out so that the instructors could teach people to play volleyball back at their own YMCAs.

The first article about the new game appeared in the July 1896 issue of the magazine *Physical Education*. The author, J. Y.

INVENTOR OF THE GAME

The child of Welsh American immigrants, William G. Morgan was born in Lockport, New York, in 1870. His parents later sent him to a private school in Massachusetts, and he graduated from Springfield College (then the YMCA Training School). There he befriended Dr. James Naismith, the clergyman who invented basketball at the college in 1891. After graduation Morgan spent a year at the Young Men's Christian Association (YMCA) in Auburn, Maine, then returned to Massachusetts, where he became a physical education director for the YMCA in Holyoke. As director, Morgan was in charge of setting up and directing exercise and sports classes for adult men at the Y.

After inventing volleyball in 1895, Morgan spent fifteen more years with the YMCA before moving back to Lockport. There he worked for the Harrison Radiator Company until he died in 1942 at age seventy-two. Throughout his life, Morgan followed the advances of the game he had invented. People who knew Morgan said that he was pleased and surprised at its popularity and that he regarded the game as belonging to athletes, not to himself as the creator.

William G. Morgan, standing at the far left, was photographed with his team in 1896.

Cameron of Buffalo, New York, declared that volleyball would "fill a place not filled by any other game" and noted the game's versatility, saying that it was "exactly adapted for the gym or . . . outdoors. Any number of people can play it."[3]

With some changes, Morgan's volleyball rules were published in 1897 when they appeared in the *Handbook of the Athletic League of the YMCAs of North America.* In the introduction to the *Handbook,* Morgan wrote:

> Volley Ball is a new game which is pre-eminently fitted for the gymnasium or the exercise hall, but which may also be played out-of-doors. Any number of persons may play the game. The play consists of keeping a ball in motion over a high net, from one side to the other, thus partaking of the character of two games—tennis and hand ball. Play is started by a player on one side serving the ball over the net into the opponent's field or court. The opponents then, without allowing the ball to strike the floor, return it, and it is in this way kept going back and forth until one side fails to return it or hits the floor. This counts a "score" for one side, or a "server out" for

> the other, depending on the side in point. The game consists of nine innings, each side serving a certain number of times, as per the rules, per inning.[4]

Morgan went on to give specific rules that told people how to play the game on a rectangular court measuring twenty-five feet by fifty feet, divided into two equal halves by a net placed six feet six inches high. However, Morgan noted that "the exact size of the court may be changed to suit the convenience of the place." He also gave precise measurements for the net, saying, "The net shall be at least two feet wide and twenty-seven feet long, and shall be suspended from uprights placed at least one foot outside the side lines."[5]

First and foremost, said Morgan, players must aim to keep the ball from touching the ground, and no player was permitted to catch or hold the ball—it must be hit back across the net or the other team would get control. Morgan's rules allowed players to hit the ball as many times as they wished before it went over the net, and players did not rotate into different positions as they do today. Instead, they played in the same place throughout the game and were expected to cover an area measuring about ten by ten feet. The team that had the most points at the end of nine innings was the winner.

Morgan also said that the innings could be organized differently, depending on how many people were playing on each side. He wrote:

> An inning consists of: when one person is playing on each side, one service each side; when two are playing on each side, two services each side; when three or more are playing on each side, three services each side. The man serving continues to do so until out by failure of his side to return the ball. Each man shall serve in turn.[6]

Under Morgan's rules, a server was allowed two tries, as in tennis. He wrote, "The server shall stand with one foot on the back line. The ball must be batted with the hand. Two services or trials are allowed him to place the ball in the opponent's court."[7] If a second serve hit the net, that was called a "foul" and the team that served it would either lose a point or forfeit the ball. As in tennis, a server could try again if the serve hit the net and still went over, but if a serve cleared the net and landed outside the boundary lines of the other court, the turn ended. Unlike tennis, a volleyball serve could land in any part of the opponent's court instead of just inside a service box.

Players were also not allowed to touch the net or encroach on areas of the opponent's court during play. If this happened, the team that did not commit the error gained control of the ball or won the point, depending on who had served. Morgan also expected people to behave politely, saying, "Any player except the captain, addressing the umpire or casting any slurring remarks at him or any of the players on the opposite side, may be disqualified, and his side be compelled to play the game without him or a substitute, or forfeit the same."[8]

Rapid Growth

Like basketball, volleyball spread from one YMCA to another, moving from New England to other states until people were playing the game all over America. Players who learned the game at their local YMCA took volleyball to their neighborhoods, schools, colleges, and even workplaces, where some people played the game during their lunch hours or organized competitive leagues to play against workers from their own or from other companies. Because people stayed within a confined court area, more than one group of players could often play at the same time in the space of one gymnasium. People also adapted the game to different circumstances. Soon people were playing it outdoors, as well as indoors, and hanging a rope at the right height if they didn't have a net.

Within ten years people in other countries also learned about volleyball, usually through the YMCA or the military. North of the border, Canadians began playing volleyball in 1900 after YMCA instructors introduced the game there, and regular intercity competitions were organized in Montreal,

A SPECIAL BALL

Since a ball was central to the game he invented, William G. Morgan experimented to find one that would work well. Basketballs were about the right size, he decided, but they were too heavy. He tried using just the inflated inner lining of the ball, called a "bladder," but it was too light. A. G. Spalding, founder of the sporting goods company A. G. Spalding and Brothers in Chicopee, Massachusetts, agreed to make a ball for Morgan, as he had done for basketball in 1894. Spalding watched some volleyball games, then went to work on the design. Like a basketball, the volleyball was made with a bladder inside but was lighter in weight. In an article called "Volley Ball Rules," written for the American Sports Publishing Company in 1917, Morgan said the new ball "gave satisfaction."

In his 1897 volleyball rules, published in the *Handbook of the Athletic League of the YMCAs of North America,* Morgan described the ball, saying, "The ball shall be a rubber bladder covered with leather or canvas. It shall measure not less than twenty-five inches, nor more than twenty-seven inches in circumference, and shall weigh not less than nine ounces nor more than twelve ounces."

Today's regulation ball is about the same size as a soccer ball, with a circumference of around twenty-six inches and a diameter slightly over eight inches. However, a volleyball is lighter and softer than a soccer ball. It weighs about nine ounces and is inflated to five to six pounds of pressure. An air-filled rubber bladder adds bounce, and leather padding on the outside makes it more comfortable to hit. The leather covering is textured, with a pattern of ten to twelve stripes, to help players control the ball.

A group of children play volleyball on their makeshift court in New York City in the 1930s.

Ottawa, and Toronto. The game also moved south to the Caribbean in 1906 when an American army officer, Agusto York, introduced the game to Cuba during a military assignment in that country.

Asians discovered volleyball next. In 1908 Hyozo Omori, a graduate of Springfield College, showed people how to play the game at the YMCA in Tokyo. Two years later YMCA representatives Max Exner and Howard Crokner brought the game to China, where people altered the rules, playing with teams of sixteen and playing to twenty-one points instead of playing nine innings.

Increasing numbers of Japanese began playing volleyball after the Reverend Frank H. Brown, an American missionary, organized teams at the Tokyo YMCA in 1913. The game was so popular that it became part of the school physical education curriculum in Japan, and students often played during recess. Adults played during breaks from work, and hundreds of volleyball teams were organized in Japanese workplaces, especially at textile companies, where most of the employees were women.

After Elwood S. (Sam) Brown, the international secretary of the YMCA, introduced volleyball in the Philippines, Filipinos built some five thousand public and private volleyball courts on their islands within a few years. In 1914, when Brown directed the Far Eastern Games in the Philippines' capital, Manila, volleyball was included as an event for the first time, with sixteen players per team.

Volleyball took hold in South America after American missionaries introduced the game in Peru in 1910. The Peruvian government had invited them to teach volleyball, basketball, and handball to schoolchildren. Although these missionaries did not teach volleyball outside Peru, people who learned to play there spread the game to Uruguay and, around 1915, to Brazil. Volleyball gained fans throughout Latin America.

While volleyball was gaining ground all over the world, the number of players was also growing in the United States. By 1916 an estimated two hundred thousand Americans were playing the game, most of them at YMCA community centers. Prevost Idell, the YMCA director in Germantown, Pennsylvania, was one of the game's strongest supporters, and he helped to organize the first Open Invitational Tournament, sponsored by the YMCA and held in Germantown.

George Fisher, the secretary of the YMCA War Office—a division that worked with the military—decided that volleyball should be part of the physical education and recreation program for U.S. soldiers. Directions for the game were included in the handbooks written for the athletics directors in charge of the army and marines. When the United States entered World War I in 1917, American troops stationed in Europe played recreational volleyball during their free time. Over sixteen thousand volleyballs and thousands of nets were given to U.S. troops and their European allies during the war, so Europeans

In 1990 American soldiers in Saudi Arabia played volleyball during their free time, just as soldiers in Europe did during World War I.

learned the game. It became especially popular in eastern Europe, where cold climates made indoor sports a practical choice. The game also spread to Africa, Egypt, and Italy, where Allied airmen played at their base in Porto Corsini. In the postwar years, Guido Graziani, a graduate of Springfield College, helped the sport to develop further in his native Italy.

The Netherlands took up the game in 1925 after a Dutch clergyman who had been living in Illinois brought the sport to a mission house in Uden and set up some courts there for players. Like so many others, Dutch players soon formed teams for people of different ages in schools and workplaces.

Rule Changes

During the game's first decades, new rules were made and the equipment was modified. These changes, which seemed to occur nearly every year, altered certain features of the court itself as well as how people played volleyball. For example, in 1906 the height of the net was raised to seven feet six inches. The length of the match was changed so that teams no longer played for nine innings. Instead, they played until one side reached twenty-one points, a number that would also vary through the years. The YMCA included these changes in its official 1906 rule book.

In 1912 the YMCA organized a special committee to make changes intended to further improve the game. The official court size was enlarged to measure thirty-five by sixty feet, and the committee specified a uniform weight and size for volleyballs: between seven and nine ounces, with a circumference of twenty-six inches. That year the number of players was set at six per side, and it was decided that players would rotate before each person took a turn serving. However, the official rule book for 1915 said that the number of players on the court could vary from two to six per team. For the first time, a definite time period was set for each game, which tended to make the game move faster. The first team to reach twenty-one points within that time period won the game, and the losing team was allowed to start serving the next game.

Several more changes took place the next year, after the National Collegiate Athletic Association (NCAA) joined the YMCA to serve as the official body governing the sport of volleyball. Together they developed new rules for men's volleyball, which were published in the Spalding Athletic Library's Blue Cover series volleyball rule book. The net height was raised to eight feet and the weight of the ball increased from eight to ten ounces. The end of a game was set at fifteen points instead of twenty-one, and a team had to win two out of three games to prevail. In addition, players were not allowed to touch the ball twice in a row. Furthermore, the *Volleyball Official Guide* stated that a player who held on to the ball would be guilty of a "foul" and would not be allowed to touch the ball until after another athlete had hit it. Players could, however, now hit the ball as low as a player's foot.

More changes occurred within the next few years. In 1920 the size of the court was changed to measure thirty by sixty feet, which remains the official size for indoor courts today. A big rule change stated that the ball could be played by any part of the body above the waist, although most players use their hands for maximum control. The number of players per team for indoor volleyball was again set at six, and in 1922 officials declared that a team could only hit the ball three times before sending it to the other side. These two rules remained in place as of 2000, although a defensive move called a block is not counted as one of the three hits.

Furthermore, players in the back line were not allowed to spike—send the ball forward and downward over the net by striking it from above with an open hand. The rules continued to ban "double hitting," which means touching the ball twice. A new scoring rule provided that if teams were tied at 14–14, a team must earn two consecutive points in order to win the game instead of just winning when they reached fifteen points.

The rules became even more specific in 1923, when they discussed player substitutes, among other things. New rules said that teams would consist of six players on the court and twelve official substitutes, and each player must wear a numbered jersey. Players on the team that had won the right to serve were to rotate clockwise, and the serve would be delivered by the player standing in the back row on the right side of the court.

The game became increasingly refined. In 1925 the official rule book allowed each team two time-outs per game. Once again the scoring rules for tie games were altered: When teams were tied at 14–14, a team no longer had to score two consecutive points to win, but they must still win by a margin of two points. In 1932 time-outs were limited to one minute.

Other changes affected the court and equipment. The 1923 rules set the ceiling height for a volleyball court at fifteen feet, minimum. In 1925 the ball weight was set at between nine to ten ounces; the next year net length was set at thirty-two feet across, making it slightly longer on each side than the thirty-foot court.

These rules were written by U.S. organizations, and some countries adopted them while others did not. When Cuba organized the first men's tournament in 1929 at the Central American and Caribbean Games, teams followed the so-called "American rules." However, in China, where volleyball was even more popular and competitive than in the United States, teams consisted of twelve players each. Later both China and Japan played with nine-person teams. Nine-person volleyball is still played in some places today.

Despite these changes, the essence of William G. Morgan's game remained: Players use their hands to serve and hit the volleyball over the net and do not have much physical contact. They aim to return the ball to the opponent's court without letting it hit the floor on their own side. After the serve is completed, play continues with the ball going back and forth until one side makes an error—for example, touches the net, double-hits the ball, or hits the ball out-of-bounds on the other side. When the ball is in play, it may hit the net but never the ground. If the serving team wins the volley, it scores one point. This method, called "side-out" scoring, prevailed for most of the twentieth century. Another method, the rally point system, awards a point to whichever team wins the volley.

Volleyball would continue to grow and change as people developed new techniques for offense and defense and as athletic organizations unified the sport and offered players more ways to compete.

Decades of Growth

Between 1920 and 1950, volleyball became a much more organized sport, both in the United States and other countries, and it gained more recognition as a competitive game. As author Steven Boga says, "Volleyball spread like a brushfire, its popularity due in part to its simplicity—few rules, few players, few basic skills, minimal equipment—and its adaptability. Players of disparate fitness levels could play on surfaces from hardwood to sand."[9]

Teams were formed at YMCAs and in academic settings, and tournaments were organized at the local, regional, and national levels. Although men's volleyball received the most attention, women also became much more involved in the sport and gained opportunities for team play and amateur competition.

As competition became more challenging, players developed new shots and strategies to improve their individual and team performance. Players from around the world contributed to the growth of the sport, as did the various organizations that were created to promote athletics and standardize the rules for national and international competition. However, although everyone played a similar game, no single set of volleyball rules emerged. Instead, rules differed slightly from one country to another and for men and women players. In the United States, different associations also developed variations of the rules for competition at the collegiate, high school, and amateur national levels.

College women played team volleyball in the 1940s.

Organized Competition

By 1920 numerous countries in Europe, Asia, and Latin America had formed volleyball leagues for both men and women in schools and workplaces, and they were holding local and even national volleyball competitions. Cuba, Japan, China, Poland, the Soviet Union, France, and Czechoslovakia were among the countries that had embraced the sport in this way and that provided opportunities for teams to compete. For example, Japan held its first high school championship in 1918, and both Czechoslovakia and Bulgaria established national volleyball federations in 1922. After the Japanese Volleyball Federation was founded in 1925, nine men's competitions were organized in that country.

Volleyball quickly became popular in the Soviet Union, where it first appeared in 1920 in cities along the Volga River and in the eastern cities of Khabarovsk and Vladivostok. By 1933 there were more than 400,000 players in the USSR and a national championship was held. When the teams from Moscow and Denpropetrovsk played a challenge match that year, they appeared at the famous Bolshoi Theatre, where the Russian ballet performs.

In the 1920s volleyball made gains in the United States as well. In 1922 the YMCA sponsored the first men's national volleyball championships at its Brooklyn Central branch in New York City. The event, which was open to YMCA teams only, drew twenty-seven teams from eleven different states and Toronto, Canada. A team from a YMCA in Pittsburgh, Pennsylvania, won the tournament and defended their title for the next three years.

Men's volleyball became part of the Amateur Athletic Union's (AAU) roster of sports. Founded in 1888 to establish standards and uniformity in amateur sports, the AAU had organized numerous other sports, including swimming and track and field, and sponsored competitions in the United States.

In 1923 the National Amateur Athletic Federation (NAAF), a major sports organization in the United States, officially recognized volleyball as a national sport. As a

A "Woman's Game," Too

Although volleyball was created for men, women quickly embraced the game, too. Their playing style differed greatly from men's during the first few decades after Morgan invented the game. During those years women wore dresses while playing sports and did not dive to the floor to retrieve the volleyball as vigorously as male players sometimes did. They played shorter, slower games.

Although women liked recreational volleyball, few women around the country played on competitive teams until after the first national volleyball championships were held in 1922. One major reason was that the game was created at the YMCA and spread primarily through that all-male organization. Also, instructional books were geared for men, and the most popular instructional book in the early 1900s was *Volley Ball, a Man's Game,* written by Robert E. Laveaga. The book strongly influenced the way people taught the game of volleyball and trained players.

Physical education instructors who did teach the game to girls recommended it primarily as a way to improve their posture and correct a condition called the "student stoop." Most people did not expect girls to play volleyball in a highly competitive way and would be amazed to see the dives, rolls, and spikes carried out by elite women volleyball players today.

result, the NAAF began organizing volleyball teams and held competitions for amateur players throughout the United States.

An increasing number of academic institutions also implemented volleyball programs. In 1923 the University of Illinois launched the first intramural volleyball program, and in 1934 the University of Washington formed the first men's varsity volleyball program that gave performance awards to its best players. As the game continued to attract more athletes, other universities launched volleyball teams. Some women's schools and colleges also sponsored volleyball teams, but more often as intramural programs instead of varsity sports.

College coaches praised volleyball and predicted it would become an important sport. During the 1920s William R. La Porte, professor of physical education at the University of Southern California, said:

> It is not difficult to foresee a very fine future for the game. . . . It has the value of co-operation to a high degree and it encourages participation under strong emotional stress. . . . We can look forward to volley ball becoming one of the most outstanding major factors in the intramural or recreational program of high school and colleges in the next few years.[10]

Seward C. Staley, professor of physical education at the University of Illinois, wrote that volleyball "has tremendous possibilities as interscholastic and intercollegiate sport. The game presents situations that are dramatic, spectacular, and thrilling to both players and spectators. It has everything that a live intercollegiate sport requires."[11]

Across the country more secondary schools made volleyball a varsity sport, usually for male students, during the 1920s and '30s. An interscholastic volleyball program was initiated at high schools in Pittsburgh, Pennsylvania, in 1923. Pennsylvania was also the first to endorse a state boys' high school volleyball championship, which debuted in 1936.

More Women Players

During the early 1900s, girls and women became increasingly involved in athletics, including team sports like volleyball. Growing numbers of women took up bowling, golf, track-and-field sports, tennis, swimming, horseback riding, and basketball.

American newspapers and magazines noticed this trend and featured articles about "the new athletic girl."[12] Unlike the pale, demure woman that had often been considered most attractive in the past, this new ideal had a rosy glow and a fit-looking body. This image was promoted through the illustrations of Charles Dana Gibson, whose "Gibson girls" appeared in *Scribner's, Harper's,* and other popular magazines during the early 1900s. Women in these illustrations wore casual blouses and skirts and were pictured

In the early 1900s "Gibson girls" wore casual clothing, making it possible for them to participate in exercise and sports.

outdoors and playing sports. Feminist Charlotte Perkins Gilman said that a Gibson girl was "braver, stronger, more healthful and skillful and able and free" than previous images of women.[13] Physical education instructors in schools and community centers began to write about the ways exercise could benefit girls and women.

Even so, many physical education experts did not think women should engage in what they considered "rough" or highly competitive sports. They encouraged women to take up activities like calisthenics, gymnastics, and dance. However, some female players and educators accepted volleyball as a woman's sport because there was little physical contact and teams were separated by a net.

After 1923 more women had a chance to play volleyball on NAAF teams organized for them. First Lady Lou Henry Hoover, an accomplished athlete herself who supported physical fitness and amateur sports for girls and women, organized and directed the women's division of the NAAF, whose slogan was "A sport for every girl, and every girl in a sport."[14]

In 1924 the first rules for women's volleyball were published in the Spalding Athletic Library's Red Cover series. Women's rules, which differed from those used in men's volleyball, called for a lower net. Instead of playing for fifteen points, the women's game was divided into halves of twenty minutes each, and the team with the most points at the end was the winner. This rule reflected the belief that women were not physically or emotionally strong enough to handle highly competitive situations—for example, when a game was tied and teams were fighting for every point.

The National Section on Women's Athletics (NSWA), a division of the American Physical Education Association (APEA), published its own set of rules for women players in 1926. NSWA rules set court dimensions at thirty by sixty feet and said that women could only touch the ball before it dropped below waist level. Ball contacts were limited to no more than three times per side.

Although more women were playing volleyball, some sportswriters did not think women had much of a future in the game or other competitive sports. The introduction to a 1928 instruction book called *Volleyball for Women* said, "The average college girl will never become an expert in the game."[15] And an article in the November 1928 issue of *Hygeia Magazine* contended that competition had an especially negative effect on women, saying, "Girls are nervously more unstable than men and are consequently more affected in the way of distraction from their studies, in the loss of sleep before and after games, and in general nervous injuries."[16]

Nonetheless, more girls and women wanted to play volleyball, and organizations responded by sponsoring teams and continuing to publish rules for them. During the 1930s the NSWA, which changed its name to the National Section for Girls' and Women's Sports (NSGWS), published a rule book for high school and college volleyball classes and intramural competition. More and more high schools and colleges included volleyball in women's physical education classes and sponsored women's teams, which played according to NSGWS rules. The sport was growing, both for men and women and for different age groups.

A National Governing Body

As more competitions were held throughout the nation, Americans began to regard volleyball as more than just recreation. By 1928 it had become so popular that a new organization, the United States Volleyball Association (USVBA), was formed to serve as the sport's national governing body. The USVBA was authorized to promote volleyball in the United States, develop uniform rules, publish an annual reference guide and official rule book, organize tournaments, certify officials, and maintain relationships with national and international sports groups. In collaboration with the YMCA, the USVBA sponsored a national championship with three men's divisions: open,

YMCA, and veterans (now called seniors). This was the first U.S. Open and the first time non-YMCA teams were invited to compete.

The AAU continued to organize its own volleyball leagues and tournaments—local, regional, and national. However, during its 1937 convention, the AAU formally agreed to recognize the U.S. Volleyball Association (USVBA) as the official national governing body for the sport.

Volleyball rules were not uniform throughout the world, but the *Annual USVBA Reference Guide* and its *Official Rules of the Game of Volleyball* became the most common reference source on the game. Other countries besides the United States looked to the USVBA for guidelines, and during World War II, thousands of the organization's rule books were circulated in various countries. Outside the United States, other countries had formed national

Volleyball for women was first introduced in physical education classes and intramural competition in the 1930s. Today, highly competitive teams are a part of many college sports programs.

volleyball associations. Three of them—Poland, France, and Czechoslovakia—were especially eager to build an international organization devoted to the sport that would standardize the rules, among other things.

Toward an International Federation

During the 1930s and '40s, people from different countries worked to unify the sport of volleyball and create an international organization. In 1934 participants at the International Handball Federation Congress in Stockholm discussed plans to begin establishing international relations in volleyball. However, their efforts came to a standstill with the onset of World War II.

Still, during World War II, volleyball moved closer to international status as U.S. troops played in more parts of the world and competed with soldiers from various countries. American soldiers played the game for fitness and recreation on training bases, in war zones, in prison camps, and even on aircraft carriers. As in World War I, U.S. officials supplied thousand of balls and nets to the military. For personnel in the South Pacific, a rope tied between trees with seawood hung from it served as a net. Army officials thought volleyball helped soldiers stay fit, improved spirits, and fostered group unity.

U.S. personnel were impressed by the way foreign soldiers played the game. Russians, Poles, Japanese, Cubans, and some others played a more rigorous, aggressive form of volleyball, diving to bring up low balls, jumping high to slam winners, and using new and more effective blocking methods in the front row at the net.

Beginning in 1943 the YMCA reached out to volleyball organizations in other countries. After Harold Friermood became secretary/treasurer of the USVBA, he worked with President Dr. George Fisher to communicate with YMCA officials in more than eighty countries. They discussed how volleyball was being played in their respective regions and talked about developing a unified approach to the game. Fisher and Friermood also stayed in contact with Polish volleyball officials, who were especially eager to support an international organization.

The Fédération Internationale de Volleyball (FIVB)

After the war volleyball matches resumed among some European nations. Then, in August 1946 representatives from the national volleyball federations of Czechoslovakia, France, and Poland met in Prague, Czechoslovakia. They drafted a document that set forth plans for what would become the Fédération Internationale de Volleyball (FIVB). It created a commission for the organization of the federation, and the three countries also declared their intention to stage a European or world championship in the near future.

In April 1947 fourteen member nations founded the FIVB, with headquarters in Paris (which moved to Lausanne, Switzerland, in 1988) and Frenchman Paul Libaud as the first president. The founding members included Brazil, Belgium, Egypt, France, Holland, Hungary, Italy, Poland, Portugal, Romania, Czechoslovakia, Yugoslavia, the United States, and Uruguay.

Representatives set out to standardize the rules. They agreed on a standard court size (21.5 by 10.67 meters) and net height (2.28 meters for men and 2.13 meters for women). At that time they settled on nine-player teams arranged equally, with three players in three lines. In 1948 the federation worked to rewrite volleyball rules so they would be more concise and easier to understand. Some rules were modified to keep pace with changes in the game, and teams that competed in FIVB events had to follow these rules.

During the next decade, other nations gradually adopted the FIVB rules and joined the organization. China began to participate in international tournaments in 1951. The Japanese Volleyball Federation agreed to accept FIVB rules in 1955 and pledged to help these rules gain acceptance throughout Asia.

The FIVB also divided the world into zones and five Continental Sport Zone Commissions were formed under its authority—Africa, Asia, Europe, South America, and NORCECA, or the North Central American and Caribbean Confederation, which included the United States, Canada, Mexico, and the Caribbean countries. In 1972 these five Sports Zone Commissions were renamed Continental Confederations. Teams in these zones competed against other member nations in certain events, and by winning certain titles, they were eligible to compete in other events.

The Fédération Internationale de Volleyball (FIVB) was founded by fourteen nations in 1947 to rewrite and standardize the rules of the game.

According to its mission statement, the FIVB aims to "govern and manage all forms of volleyball and beach volleyball worldwide, through planning, organising, marketing and promotional activities aimed at developing volleyball as a major world sport."[17] As the international governing body for the sport, the FIVB periodically issues new rules to resolve debates and to address new kinds of playing techniques, as well as to clarify its regulations. For example, by the time the FIVB was founded in 1947, players had devised new ways to block offensive shots, so the FIVB gave "blocking" a more precise definition. They also focused on the serving process, stating that a player must serve only in the right third of the backcourt boundary and that the other players must be standing in their correct places during the service.

Now that the sport had become more unified under the FIVB, more international volleyball matches could be held, based on a common set of rules. FIVB representatives created or modified rules at their annual congresses, where they covered many different aspects of the game, such as shot making, court movement, fouls, and officiating. In 1956 the FIVB began publishing its official bulletin to update members on events and other developments.

Active National Organizations

While the FIVB was promoting volleyball internationally, new national organizations were being formed and existing national organizations were expanding to keep pace with the growth of volleyball. For example, the Brazilian Confederation of Desportos, the body that controlled volleyball in that nation, sponsored the first South American championship, for both men and women, in September 1951, in Rio de Janeiro. The Brazilian men's and women's teams won both events.

"HOOVER-BALL"

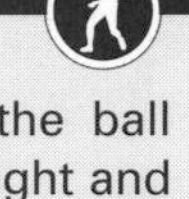

In 1931 a White House physician named Joel T. Boone combined elements of volleyball, tennis, and medicine ball to create a game to help President Herbert Hoover stay fit. Hoover had enjoyed playing a game called bull-in-the-ring while on board a naval ship in 1928, and his physician was inspired to develop a different type of medicine-ball game for Hoover. When a reporter wrote about the game in the *New York Times Magazine,* he called it "Hoover-Ball" and the name stuck.

To play, teams of two to four people served, caught, and threw a six-pound medicine ball over a net placed eight feet high on a court that resembled a tennis court. Teams scored when they threw the ball back in a way that could not be caught and returned or when an opponent threw a ball out-of-bounds. The president and four to eighteen other men, known as the "Medicine Ball Cabinet," assembled for the game around 7 A.M. each morning except Sunday.

Dr. Boone claimed his game was more strenuous than many other sports, including football, and was designed to give the president a vigorous workout in a short amount of time. In his *Memoirs,* Hoover later wrote, "It required less skill than tennis, was faster and more vigorous, and therefore gave more exercise in a short time."

In some countries the YMCA continued to play a key role in the sport it had launched in the 1890s. Charles Pegg, the national physical education director for YMCA in Great Britain, helped to create the Amateur Volleyball Association of Great Britain and Northern Ireland in 1955. The first National Festival of Volleyball was held at the London YMCA the following year.

In the United States the USVBA, which had joined the FIVB, continued to carry out many activities on behalf of volleyball. The postwar years brought more new players, including military veterans who formed college club teams and requested varsity programs as they took advantage of the government's GI Bill to pursue higher education. Numerous colleges and universities added volleyball programs. In 1949 Florida State University became the first college in America to hire a full-time volleyball coach and offer men volleyball scholarships.

That same year, for the first time the USVBA began holding an annual championship tournament for women as part of its national Open Championships. The USVBA sponsored a men's team for the second men's World Championships, held in 1952, and sent a women's team to the first World Championships for women. It would also help to sponsor U.S. teams that participated in the Pan American Games and Olympic Games, after volleyball became part of those competitions. At the college level, the USVBA established the National Collegiate Championships for men and supervised those tournaments until 1969, when the National Collegiate Athletic Association (NCAA) assumed that role.

These kinds of activities, both on the national and international level, gave athletes more chances to play volleyball, both for fun and in competition. Wherever it was played, volleyball was much more sophisticated than it had been a few decades earlier.

A More Competitive Game

The growth of international competition and years of experience with the sport made volleyball a far more competitive sport. By the 1950s volleyball players were no longer just trying to bat the ball back over the net. Instead, they were thinking strategically and using complex offensive and defensive means to defeat their opponents. With just three opportunities to hit the ball on their side, they had to make every shot count, then respond quickly to whatever their opponents sent over the net.

One major innovation was the "set and spike." This offensive technique for passing and hitting the ball was first seen in 1916 in the Philippines and dubbed the "Filipino Bomb." One player hit the ball so that it was in a good position for another player to spike it firmly into the opposite court. The attack or spike shot—sending the ball forward and downward over the net by striking it with an open hand overhead—remains one of the most powerful offensive plays in volleyball.

A player delivers a masterful "bump" in a state volleyball championship game.

To combat the spike, players in the front row on the opposite side began trying to block the shot as it came over, sending it right back to their opponents. Blocking enabled them to avoid having to return some potentially lethal shots. During the 1930s the Czechs were known for their skill at blocking, and the Russians also excelled in these defensive moves. In 1938 the USVBA made rules that specifically addressed blocking, which was defined as "a counteraction at the net by one or two adjacent players."[18]

Players also learned to "bump," getting down under the ball with both hands joined and their arms in a V shape in order to propel the ball upward to a place where another player could hit it. When using the bump pass, a player passed or set the ball in an underhanded fashion.

People also became more aggressive in retrieving serves and spikes. To keep balls from hitting the floor, players and coaches used defensive moves, including the "dig"—slang for the process of rescuing a spiked ball that landed close to the floor.

As the game became more complex, players began to specialize in a certain role, such as hitter, spiker, digger, or blocker. Other players became setters, who positioned the ball high in the air in position for a spike. Players became adept at their various roles and in more than one capacity as they practiced these moves and used them in competition to improve the overall performance of the team.

Some of the elements William G. Morgan had built into his game in 1895 endured and strongly influenced the development of volleyball: Players hit the ball with their hands and tried to get it back over the net into the opponent's court without letting it touch the floor on their side. Team members had to work together in a relatively small space. These features made volleyball "a game of rebound and movement," as authors Darlene A. Kluka and Peter J. Dunn explain:

> The ball is never motionless from the moment it is served until it contacts the floor or is whistled dead by an official. . . . The size of the court is relatively small for the number of players. . . . Because of this, the game has evolved into one of efficiency, accuracy, and supportive movements.[19]

By the 1950s athletes and coaches had found innovative ways to thwart their opponents. They became more efficient and accurate and learned to maximize their movements as a team. The stage was set for vigorous global competition, as volleyball evolved into the action-packed game that elite athletes play today.

A Global Competitive Sport

By the 1950s volleyball had achieved the status of a national sport in numerous countries, with a national governing body and organized championships. During the last half of the twentieth century, volleyball achieved recognition as an international sport, with worldwide competitions for amateur and professional players and Olympic status for men and women in both indoor and beach volleyball. While a few nations dominated international competition during the 1950s and '60s, new stars emerged later in the century, and teams from the United States, the birthplace of the sport, finally captured their first Olympic medals during the 1980s.

International Championships

The FIVB fulfilled its 1947 pledge to sponsor international tournaments for both men and women. In 1949 men from different countries competed in Prague, where the FIVB held its first men's World Championships, and a superb Soviet team won the crown that year. The Soviets displayed impressive teamwork and accurate spikes. During this tournament they launched a new technique in which a setter penetrated from the back line, leading to a three-player attack. The first women's World Championship tournament took place in 1952 in Moscow, where the "hometown" team, the USSR, won the women's title. The World Championships continued to grow so that by 1956 twenty-four men's teams from four continents competed for the men's title.

The year 1960 marked the first time the World Championships were played outside of Europe. At this event, held in Brazil, the USSR men's team took top honors; the Russian women also won the World Championships that year. Two years later the USSR men's team won the World Championships again, in Moscow. However, the Japanese women won a surprise victory that year, the first time they had clinched a World Championship. They amazed spectators with their talent and tenacity, both that year and when they won again in 1967.

While some countries invariably sent strong teams, different teams sometimes emerged triumphant through the years. At the 1978 World Championships in Rome, the USSR men's team defeated Italy in the semifinals, but the women, who played in Leningrad, crowned a new winner when Cuba won its first world title in the sport. The Japanese and the Soviet women's teams

Beach volleyball has blossomed into an international Olympic sport.

filled the other top spots. China's women's team enjoyed its first victory in 1982, when the World Championships were held in Peru.

In 1990 Italy upset Cuba in Rio de Janeiro and became the first western European country to win the men's volleyball World Championships. Italy won the men's title for the second consecutive time in 1994. At the women's World Championships in Brazil, twenty-six thousand spectators—the highest number ever to watch a women's event—came out for the matches. The Cuban women captured the World Championship title in 1994.

Another major competition, the volleyball World Cup, was launched in 1965, and the Soviet men's team won the first competition, which was held in Poland. In Berlin, East Germany won the second men's World Cup. The first women's World Cup, won by the Soviet team, was played in Uruguay in 1973. The World Cup became an annual event for both men and women, and in 1977 the championships were situated permanently in Japan. That year the Soviet men and the Japanese women took top honors.

New kinds of international tournaments were introduced during the 1980s and 1990s as volleyball continued to gain new fans around the world. In 1992 the World Grand Champions Cup was launched. This event is played every four years in Japan, alternating on odd years with the World Cup. The first teams to win the World Grand Champions Cup were Italy (men) and Cuba (women).

In 1985 the World Gala debuted, with an All-Star team made up of top players from around the world challenging the Olympic gold medal–winning team. The World Gala is an event for both men and women and is held in the year following each Olympic Games. The 1995 World Gala was a special event, taking place on the hundredth anniversary of the game of volleyball. That year the Italian men's team defeated the All-Stars and received the Centennial Cup from International Olympic Committee (IOC) President Juan Antonio Samaranch.

Regional championships have also flourished. In the Western Hemisphere, teams from North, Central, and South America competed in the Pan American Games, which added men's volleyball as a sport in 1955 when the games were held in Mexico City. In 1963 women's volleyball was added. The first Asian Games were played in Tokyo in 1955, with tournaments for both six-player and nine-player teams, and it remains a popular annual event. Regional tournaments were also organized in Africa. However, volleyball had yet to be added to the Olympics.

Road to the Olympics

Many people worked for years to make volleyball an Olympic sport. At the 1924 Olympic Games in Paris, volleyball was included in a demonstration of American sports, but forty years would pass before teams played for Olympic medals. Official

Brazil won the women's competition in the 1999 Pan American Games in Winnipeg, Canada.

records show that in 1925 the IOC was asked to consider adding volleyball to the Olympics, but at that time there was no official international volleyball organization, a requirement for inclusion in the Olympics. The formation of the FIVB in 1947 was a key step in the inclusion process.

In 1957, at a meeting in Bulgaria, the IOC finally agreed to include volleyball as an official Olympic team sport. However, more issues still had to be settled before it debuted at the Summer Games. The FIVB proceeded to create an official score sheet and a plan for certifying volleyball scores

The U.S. men's team traveled to Tokyo, Japan, in 1964 to participate in the first Olympic competition.

and timers that would be used in the competition. The federation also voted to adopt the U.S. plan of codifying rules.

In 1962 it became official: the IOC announced that both women's and men's volleyball would be on the program for the 1964 Olympic Games, scheduled to take place in Tokyo, Japan. The 1964 games had a special political significance because it was the first time any Asian country had ever hosted an Olympics. Japanese officials had carefully planned the Olympics and spent millions of dollars on the facilities. The nation was proud of its athletes, including its volleyball teams, and had high hopes of winning at least one Olympic medal in the newly admitted sport.

Olympic Debut

When the first Olympic volleyball matches began in Tokyo on October 13, ten men's teams and six women's teams were in competition. To qualify for the games, a team had to place either first or second in one of the major international tournaments, such as the World Championships, Pan American Games, or European Championships.

The men's matches were hard fought, with the Soviet team winning and Czechoslovakia capturing a second-place silver medal. They demonstrated the dazzling moves that had made these two teams so difficult to defeat and that had made the Soviets dominant in world competition for many years. The Japanese men's team won the third-place bronze medal.

However, the women's matches were among the most dramatic of the games and have become part of Olympic legend. The Japanese women's team had trained rigorously for the games with their coach, Hirofumi Daimatsu. They had mastered the sport so thoroughly that they won every match during the games, except for one set against Poland, the eventual bronze medalists. During that set Daimatsu removed his best players so the Soviet team would not see them in action. The dramatic finale between Japan and the Soviet Union was one of the highest-rated television events in Japanese history, viewed by 80 percent of that day's audience. When they won the match, the Japanese women became national heroes and the press called them "Wizards of the Orient." Daimatsu, who quit coaching volleyball after the games, was elected to the Japanese parliament four years later.

Not to be outdone, the Soviet women's team won gold at the next two Olympics, in 1968 and 1972. At the 1968 games, held in Mexico City, when the USSR team played their final match against the Czech women's team, they were booed because of politics: Two months before the Olympics, the Soviet government had sent tanks to repress rebellion in Czechoslovakia, a country it had occupied since the end of World War II. Despite this negative reception, the team triumphed. The final match in Munich in 1972 included a thrilling fourth set in which Russia and Japan served a total of twenty-four times without anyone scoring a point. After five grueling sets, the Soviet women won another Olympic gold medal.

The Soviet men's team also prevailed in 1968, defeating the silver medalist, Japan, in a four-set final. During that tournament the Soviet men lost only one game while playing the United States at the start of the Olympics. Although the U.S. men only placed seventh overall, their victory against the Soviets bolstered their hopes for future success.

Hirofumi Daimatsu led his Japanese women's team to victory in the 1964 Olympic Games. That gold-medal match with the USSR is one of the highest-rated television events in Japanese history.

Stiff Competition

Between 1964 and 1988, teams from the Soviet Union continued to dominate volleyball and won at least one medal in every Olympics, including several gold medals. Japan, China, Czechoslovakia, and Poland were also known for their outstanding players. However, as other nations built stronger teams, new Olympic champions emerged, just as they were claiming top prizes in other tournaments, such as the World Championships and World Cup.

During the 1970s and '80s, international politics sometimes affected volleyball competition. In 1971 the U.S. State Department permitted the men's volleyball team to go to Cuba, a nation that had adopted a communist form of government in 1959 under dictator-president Fidel Castro. The United States had suspended diplomatic relations with Cuba in the early 1960s and banned U.S. citizens from traveling freely to Cuba without special permission from the U.S. government. In this case, the two teams had to play a match that would determine which country would represent North America at the 1972 Olympics. The Cubans were favored.

When the match began, according to sports historian George Gipe, the 16,500 spectators in the Sports Coliseum in Havana heard Cuban dictator Fidel Castro "lambaste the United States, then turn abruptly generous, [saying], 'We shouldn't consider these athletes as representatives of imperialism. Rather we should look on them as representatives of the United States.'"[20] The Cuban team lost some ground when the U.S. team won the first game in only nineteen minutes. However, they recovered to win the next three games, take the match, and proceed to the Olympics.

VOLLEYBALL ON STAMPS

Through the years at least 151 countries have issued stamps featuring players, balls, or designs incorporating a volleyball theme. The first volleyball-related postage stamp was produced by Romania in 1945. Since then, many of the stamps have commemorated a particular Olympic Games, such as the one issued by Spain in 1992 when Barcelona hosted the games, or other special occasions, such as the hundredth anniversary of the game. Volleyball stamps have come from diverse places, including Cuba, Paraguay, San Marino, Slovakia, Yugoslavia, Italy, Central Africa, and the Soviet Union. As of 2000 there were more than a thousand different stamps with volleyball subjects, and some people specialize in collections featuring the sport. In 2001 the Chinese government announced that it would feature thirty-six sports and entertainment stars on a series of new stamps to support Beijing's bid to host the 2008 Olympics. Lang Ping, one of China's greatest volleyball players and coaches, appears on one of the new stamps.

At those games the Japanese men's team, which had previously won bronze and silver medals, finally captured gold in Munich. The speed and agility of their top playmakers, such as Katsutoshi Nekoda, and skillful management by coach Yasutaka Matsudaira, were instrumental in the team's success. The Soviet women won the gold medal.

After winning the gold at the Los Angeles Olympics in 1984, the U.S. men's team celebrated their achievement on the medal stand.

Poland won its first gold medal in volleyball in 1976 when their national men's team toppled the competition. To prepare for the Olympics, the Polish national team had tried a new kind of strength training that involved jumping over a 4.5-foot barrier hundreds of times while wearing twenty- to thirty-pound weights on their arms and legs. They needed their strength and endurance, with three of their first five matches going a full five sets. In a thrilling match against Cuba, they won the last set, 20–18. In the final they defeated the USSR, after coming from behind, two sets to one, with the Soviets ahead 15–14 in the fourth set. After rallying to a 19–17 win, they took the fifth and final set, 15–7.

The Soviet men, who had long dominated the sport, were disappointed to finish third in 1972 and second in 1976. Determined to regain the top spot, they embarked on a strenuous training regime for the 1980 games. For political reasons, U.S. volleyball teams did not compete at all in those Olympics. After the Soviet Union invaded Afghanistan, President Jimmy Carter decided that the United States would boycott the Moscow Olympics in protest. There, the Soviet men won their third gold medal in volleyball and were undefeated during the entire Olympics. The Soviet women's team also struck gold.

In response to the U.S. boycott, Soviet athletes and their allies, the Cubans, did not participate in 1984 when the Olympics were held in Los Angeles. China had not participated in the Olympics for thirty-two years, and their women's volleyball team won the gold medal, with the U.S. women taking the silver. The Brazilian men, who won the silver

THE LONGEST MATCH IN NCAA HISTORY

In 1998 two women's collegiate teams played the longest match in the history of the NCAA: three hours and thirty-eight minutes. The scene was at the MGM Grand Garden Arena in Las Vegas, Nevada, where the University of Hawaii Rainbow Wahine played five grueling sets with the Brigham Young Cougars to finally prevail 15–12, 21–19, 13–15, 16–18, 24–22.

During the hard-fought match, the Wahine's senior outside hitter Leah Karratti racked up twenty-three kills, including the one that ended the match, while the team's middle hitter Veronica Lima completed a total of seventeen kills. Karratti and setter Nikki Hubbert won many decisive points. Combined, the two teams broke eleven Western Athletic Conference (WAC) tournament records, including the national record for the most points ever scored in a game—eighty-nine points for UH.

The two teams had met before in the WAC finals, and the Cougars defeated UH in both 1996 and '97. In an interview with *College Sports News,* Hawaii's head coach Dave Shoji said, "We were very fortunate to be part of one of the greatest matches I've ever seen. I don't think you're ever going to see another match like that."

medal, impressed the crowds with their effective jumping serves.

At the 1988 Olympics in Seoul, Korea, the Peruvian women's team, featuring six feet five inch middle blocker Gabriela Perez del Solar, was a strong contender for the first time. As they had done for years, Japan, China, and the Soviet Union sent outstanding teams. In the semifinal match, the Peruvians were down in the fifth set, 9–14, yet they managed to score seven consecutive points to get to the finals. During this dramatic competition, each team won two sets, and the fifth and final set was hard fought. Twice the Soviets led by several points, but the Peruvian women managed to tie the score. After several match points, the Soviet women won 17–15 for a three-set victory and Peru took home a silver medal, its first volleyball medal.

One of the most formidable teams of the twentieth century made its debut at the 1992 Olympics. The Cuban women managed to defeat a talented group of Americans in the semifinals during five difficult sets. They recovered from seven ties to win the last game and earn a berth in the finals, where they defeated the Unified Team, made up of players from the former Soviet Union. U.S. women took home the bronze. The Cuban women went on to win an unprecedented three gold medals in successive Olympics—1992, '96, and 2000.

U.S. Men Triumph

As of 1980, despite the long history of volleyball in the United States, no U.S. team had won an Olympic medal. In 1964 the U.S. men had finished ninth; four years later they finished seventh while the women's team finished eighth. At some Olympics U.S. teams did not even qualify.

However, more outstanding players were emerging. Collegiate programs were improving throughout the nation. More Americans were also playing competitive volleyball at younger ages, thanks to a growing number of programs in schools and communities, including the Junior Olympics. The USVBA also set up a year-round training program for the national men's team in Ohio in 1977; in 1981 it was moved to San Diego, California.

These developments contributed greatly to the team's success during the 1980s, according to authors Darlene Kluka and Peter Dunn:

> Many believe the primary contributing factors included a full-time training center and a unique style of play. By studying American characteristics and philosophy, members of the national training center staff created an approach to the game that was uniquely "American." It involved a strong offense, based

The Cuban women's team made their Olympic debut in 1992 by winning the gold medal. In 2000 they celebrated with their coach after capturing their third consecutive Olympic gold.

> upon an attack from the inside working out, and a defense that combined agility with power.[21]

In 1984 the U.S. men's team—which included such outstanding athletes as Karcsi (Karch) Kiraly and Dusty Dvorak—won twenty-four consecutive matches, each time outside the United States, including four victories over the reigning world champions, the Soviets. The Americans were eager to bring home an Olympic medal. They faced a tough Brazilian team in the finals but managed to win their match in straight games: 15–6, 15–6, 15–7. Finally, the United States had a volleyball medal—and it was the gold.

The team repeated its triumph four years later when it won a second gold at the Olympics in Seoul, Korea. In the final round they faced the Soviet team, which had not competed four years earlier in Los Angeles. The match began with each team winning a game, but the U.S. men proceeded to win the next two for a three-out-of-four victory. From 1984 to 1988, the U.S. men's volleyball team was considered the best in the world. For the first time, the team won the "Triple Crown" of volleyball—the Olympics, World Cup, and World Championships—in 1984, '85, and '86, respectively.

In 1992 at Barcelona, the U.S. men won another medal, this time the bronze, while Brazil earned its first gold and the men's team from the Netherlands won the silver. U.S. men's coach Fred Sturm later said, "Brazil was the hottest team in the tournament. They were on fire and almost impossible to beat."[22] The 1992 Olympics marked the first time the Soviet men failed to win a medal.

Medals for U.S. Women

The U.S. women's team also won its first Olympic medal during the 1980s. In 1984 they won the silver medal in Los Angeles, and they won a bronze medal in 1992 at the Barcelona Olympics.

Several factors contributed to their increasing success in competition. More American women had begun playing volleyball at earlier ages and were taking part in programs sponsored by the Association of Intercollegiate Athletics for Women (AIAW), which sponsored women's national championships from 1970–81 until the NCAA took over in 1982. The NCAA also covered the travel expenses of participants, which made it possible for more women to play in more challenging events.

Changes in the law also gave American girls more opportunities to play volleyball and other sports. Title IX, a federal law enacted in 1972, states: "No person in the United States shall, on the basis of sex, be excluded from participation in, be denied the benefits of, or be subjected to discrimination under any educational program or activity, receiving federal financial assistance."[23] This meant that public educational facilities must

Title IX, a federal law enacted in 1972, requires the funding for women's athletics to be equal to that of the men. The resulting interscholastic volleyball programs have brought women to the highest competitive levels.

allocate funding for women's sports in order to bring them in line with the funding that men's programs received.

As a result, the number of high schools offering interscholastic volleyball competition for girls increased from 3,312 in 1968 to 11,690 in 1978. During those years the number of female volleyball players rose from 59,132 to 326,091. The number of high school championships also rose accordingly. After the 1970s more American women grew up playing volleyball and were better prepared to play in international competition.

Training improved the performance of the women's national team as it had for the

U.S. men. In 1975 a full-time, year-round training program was set up for the national team, first in Texas, then in Colorado Springs in 1979. During the 1980s the program was moved to San Diego and combined with the program for male athletes.

Arie Selinger coached the U.S. women's national team from 1975 to 1984, building it into one of the world's best teams and Olympic silver medalists. In his book *Power Volleyball,* he describes the approach he used as a coach to develop what he calls "a distinctive American style of play":

Arie Selinger, through creative new approaches to the game, coached the U.S. women's team to world-class status in the early 1980s.

> I see volleyball as a game of expectations, a game played primarily in emergency situations. Whereas many coaches tend to emphasize the most stable body positions for the execution of the fundamental skills, I emphasize the execution of skills in motion in the least stable body position. For me, the realization that volleyball is a geometrical game of angles led to the development of many unconventional techniques.[24]

Creative new approaches to the game, like those developed by Selinger and other top coaches, have helped players to develop new skills and enabled both amateurs and professionals to play the dynamic game that evolved in the last decades of the twentieth century.

Professional Volleyball

Before 1975 indoor volleyball remained a mostly amateur sport in the United States, but that year professional volleyball became a reality when the International Volleyball Association (IVA) was formed. Its teams, composed of both men and women, were based largely in cities in the Southwest and West Coast, including Los Angeles and Phoenix. Men and women had slightly different roles during the match, with women playing defensive positions and men taking more offensive responsibilities. The IVA attracted some "name" players, including basketball great Wilt Chamberlain, who enjoyed playing

TOP MEDALISTS: SOVIET TEAMS

The Soviet Union/Russia has produced some of the finest volleyball teams in history. In addition to many regional, European, and international titles, they hold the record for Olympic medals: their men's teams won gold in 1964, '68, and '80, silver in '76 and '88, and bronze in '72; women's teams earned gold in 1968, '72, '80, and '88 and silver in '64 and '76. After the USSR was reorganized, the women's Unified Team from former Soviet countries won a silver medal in 1992; Russian men's and women's teams won silver medals in 2000.

Outstanding players have propelled these teams to victory. One of them, Inna Ryskal, was among three women nominated by the FIVB as the best woman player of the twentieth century. From 1964 to 1976, Ryskal was one of the world's top players, and some experts call her the best left attacker ever to play women's volleyball. As of 2000 Ryskal was the only woman in history to win four Olympic medals for volleyball: silver in 1964 and '76 and gold in '68 and '72. Among the men, Hall of Famer Yuri Tchesnokov—a player, coach, and administrator during his long career—was one of the world's best blockers and spikers when he played on the Soviet team and won his gold medal in 1964.

In a 1999 interview for *Volleyball Online Magazine,* Nikolai Karpol, who began coaching the women's team in 1969, said the Russian training system has sparked their success. Karpol said training includes sprints and some long-distance running, basketball, soccer, and acrobatics. He explained that basketball and soccer are for "changing the mood, for getting game sense, and for bring[ing] up the flexibility of body and brain to think which could correspond to various kinds of situations in [the] game."

volleyball after he retired from competitive basketball. However, the league struggled financially and was disbanded in 1982.

In the United States a women's professional league, the Major League Volleyball organization (MLV), was set up in 1987. Like the IVA, the MLV struggled to attract enough fans, television coverage, and sponsors, folding in 1989. One longstanding problem with television coverage is that the time of a match can vary, lasting from about one hour to over three hours. For that reason, networks were often reluctant to cover matches in their entirety.

Although these attempts to form professional indoor volleyball leagues did not succeed in the United States, some countries, such as Italy and Japan, have developed strong professional teams where volleyball players can earn a living at their sport. A number of players from around the world have spent time playing pro volleyball in these countries. They include Olympic gold medalists Karch Kiraly, Bob Samuelson, and Flo Hyman.

In 1990 the formation of the men's World League brought new opportunities to win money—the league offered $1 million in prizes that first year. Teams competing in the championship had to first qualify, then participate in direct elimination matches right up to the finals to determine first through

In his book, Power Volleyball, Coach Arie Selinger emphasizes the execution of skills in motion.

eighth places. A crowd of ten thousand spectators watched as Italy won the first World League in Tokyo, Japan.

Italy also won the second World League event, which featured $2 million in prize money for the teams. The final took place in Milan, where twelve thousand spectators watched the home team defeat Cuba. When the third World League was staged in 1992, the prize money increased to $3 million, and once again the Italian men's team won, in its final match against the Netherlands.

A women's version of the World League, the Grand Prix, was launched in 1993, with $1 million in prizes. Matches were played in Asia, and the Cuban team defeated China in the finals. Brazil captured the men's title when the World League final was held that year in São Paulo, Brazil. By 1994 the purse at the fifth edition of the men's World League was up to $6 million. Italy regained its title, defeating Cuba.

Aside from these special events, money-making opportunities for indoor volleyball players have been limited in the United States. Top beach volleyball players have had more chances to earn money in their sport.

Beach Volleyball

"It's ninety degrees. The ocean is thirty feet away; friends and fans surround the court. I hardly notice."[25] Gabrielle Reece is too busy concentrating on the volleyball match she is playing—outdoors on the beach rather than on an indoor court. Reece is a world-class beach volleyball player and the author of a book about her sport.

Since people began playing beach volleyball in southern California in the 1920s, this sport has gained fans around the world and players have found increasing opportunities to compete as amateurs and professionals. At the first pro tournament, teams played for a prize of soft drinks; by 2001 pro beach volleyball players were vying each year for millions of dollars in prize money. Top players can now participate in events for men's, women's, and coed teams. Recreational play is on the rise, too, and some clubs and resorts bring sand into their facilities so that people can enjoy the game.

The game, which became an Olympic sport in 1996, offers some special challenges, and two-person teams must cover more ground than they would on an indoor team. While some athletes specialize in beach volleyball, still others have excelled at both the outdoor and indoor game. One of the best is Liz Masakayan, who was a two-time NCAA All-American before becoming a top beach volleyball player. Masakayan says, "The success of the two-person team requires trust, responsibility, and problem-solving. . . . The key is to stay focused, play with confidence, and have patience."[26]

A New Kind of Volleyball

Although volleyball was invented as an indoor sport that people could play during the winter months, it quickly spread outdoors to parks and playgrounds and then to the beach. Like indoor volleyball, beach volleyball originated in North America, but on the opposite coast. Most accounts state that beach volleyball was first played in California during the 1920s. During that decade people set up volleyball nets on the beach at Santa Monica, California, and families played in teams of six.

The game naturally became most popular in beach communities, and people were soon playing in Hawaii and Florida, as well as other places. Besides seaside beaches, the game was played on sandy areas around lakes. By 1927 beach volleyball games were also taking place in France outside of Paris. Within ten years people in other parts of France and in Bulgaria, Prague, and Latvia were playing volleyball on the beach, too. During the Great Depression of the 1930s, volleyball was a relatively inexpensive form of entertainment and more American families in California began playing the game, with teams numbering three to four players each.

In the early years people played outdoor volleyball by the same rules as they did indoors, but the rules changed somewhat over

People have been playing volleyball on the beaches of southern California since the 1920s.

"QUEEN OF THE BEACH": PLAYER AND COACH KATHY GREGORY

Winner of the Women's Beach Tournament Player of the Year title in 1976, '77, '78, '81, and '83, Kathy Gregory became known as the "Queen of the Beach." As a player and coach, the 1989 U.S. Volleyball Hall of Fame inductee is considered to be one of the ten people who most influenced volleyball during the late twentieth century.

A native of Santa Barbara, California, Gregory was a member of the U.S. team that competed in the 1968 Olympics, a pro with the San Diego Breakers of the IVA, and a member of the U.S. Pan American and World Games teams. Gregory was named MVP four times and All-American fifteen times. In 1975 she became coach of the University of California–Santa Barbara's first varsity women's volleyball team and attained a career record of 599 wins, 263 losses during a twenty-three-year period. During the 1993 season, when the team posted a 28-4 record and finished fourth in the nation, Gregory received the AVCA/Tachikara National Coach of the Year award. As of 2000 she was also one of only five women coaches nominated for the Women's Sports Foundation Hall of Fame, in honor of her outstanding contribution to women's athletics. Commenting on her approach in the UCSB faculty catalog, Gregory says, "I teach my players to be independent and self-reliant, and to face adversity."

During the 1990s, Gregory continued to play beach volleyball and in 1996 was the most senior player in the nation to achieve the AAA beach ranking—the top rating for a beach player. That year she and her partner Kathy Hanley won the Santa Barbara Bud Light tournament.

time. Beach players still cannot double-touch the ball or hit it more than three times to get it back over the net, but the number of players per side is usually two rather than six. Players also move differently on the court than they do in indoor volleyball. Indoor teams rotate players into six different positions on the front and rear court and substitutes are permitted. However, in the beach game, two players must cover the whole court with no substitutions, so each player hits the ball more often than indoor players. Games go to twelve points instead of fifteen, and, unlike indoor volleyball, the court is not divided into a front court and back. The net height is eight feet. In addition, beach players must move on sand, not a hard surface, so jumping requires more effort. Sun, wind, and other weather conditions can also affect the game. These features add excitement both for players and fans.

Early Competition

The first two-man beach volleyball game probably took place in Santa Monica, California, around 1930. Seventeen years later the first two-man beach tournament took place at Will Rogers State Beach near Santa Monica, but no prizes were offered. At a tournament held the next year in Los Angeles, the winners did receive a prize—a case of Pepsi-Cola.

By the 1950s a tournament circuit had been organized on five California beaches—at Will Rogers State Beach, Corona Del Mar, Laguna Beach, and at San Diego and Santa Barbara beaches. Local Parks and Recreation Departments in these places were in charge of the circuit. Beach volleyball tournaments were also being organized in other countries during that decade. Brazil held its first official tournament, sponsored by a newspaper company.

Showmanship played a large role in the early tournaments. During the 1950s entertainment and beauty contests were often held along with the athletic competition, and actresses and models presided as "Queen of the Beach." The mood at the tournaments was often relaxed, with players competing in their swimsuits and people jumping into the ocean to cool off after a match. However, the competition was keen. Top players of the '50s included Eugene (Gene) Selznick, one of the best players on the California circuit. The team of Bernie Holtzman and Manny Saenez won numerous titles.

The number of tournaments continued to grow during the 1960s as more California beaches became part of the volleyball circuit. In 1960 the first Manhattan Beach Open was held. Beach volleyball tournaments became popular in other countries, too, including France, where players competed for a top prize of about thirty thousand francs in tournaments that were held in La Baule and in Les Sables-d'Olonne.

During 1965 and 1966, Gene Selznick paired with Ron Von Hagen and Ron Lang, respectively, to win more beach volleyball tournaments than any other player. Other top players during the 1960s were Mike O'Hara, Mike Bright, Henry Bergman, and Larry Rundle. Bergmen and Rundle, who won more beach tournaments than any other team in 1969, continued to dominate men's events during the early 1970s. They encountered stiff competition from the team of Ron Von Hagen and Ron Lang, who also won many matches during the late '60s and early '70s. Von Hagen, who has been called the "Babe Ruth of Beach Volleyball," retired in 1976 with sixty-two open victories, a record at that time.

During the late 1970s players Jim Menges, Greg Lee, Matt Gage, and Dane Selznick won numerous tournaments. Playing with three different partners, Jim Menges achieved more tournament victories than any other player in four different years: 1975, '76, '77, and '79.

Tournaments Gain Commercial Sponsors

Beach volleyball thrived during the 1970s when an increasing number of tournaments were held, drawing more players and spectators. Some tournaments were sponsored by large companies, which enabled some top players to earn a living through their sport. The first commercially backed event was the San Diego Open of 1974, sponsored

Eugene "Gene" Selznick was one of the top players on the beach volleyball circuit in the 1950s. He has been inducted into the Volleyball Hall of Fame.

by Winston cigarettes. Dennis Hare and Fred Zuelich won first prize before a crowd of 250 people. Just two years later, when the team of Jim Menges and Greg Lee won the Olympia Championship of 1976 before thirty thousand spectators, they took home $5,000.

Still, most beach volleyball tournaments remained fairly low-key during the early to mid-1970s, and many continued to stage beauty contests and other nonathletic events. Legendary player Karch Kiraly recalls, "It was just you and your partner, you're just wearing a pair of shorts and you were just trying to win a trophy or a six-pack of soda or a beach chair."[27] Another beach volleyball star, Sinjin Smith, says, "In the mid-to-late '70s, there was no media attention, no bleachers, no signage, no sponsors, but there'd be 10,000 people watching. That was awesome, it was unbelievable. Ten thousand people watching four guys in the sand."[28]

In 1978 Jose Cuervo Tequila signed as the first major sponsor for the beach volleyball circuit, and prize money increased each year as more sponsors funded tournaments. Winners of the 1979 Open were awarded $10,000, and the next year's King of the Beach winners took home $11,000. Jose Cuervo provided a total of $52,000 for the winners of seven 1980 tournaments, including San Diego, Santa Barbara, Laguna, Manhattan, King of the Beach ($12,000), and the World Championships ($15,000).

Prize totals rose still higher in the 1980s when the beach volleyball tournament went national, beginning with the Clearwater (Florida) Open of 1982. That year the Miller Brewing Company sponsored the tour, which offered $69,000 in total cash prizes. The next year Miller again sponsored the tour, and the prizes reached $137,000. Four states—New York, Colorado, Florida, and California—were part of the circuit, and that number increased to seven states the next year when events in Illinois, Arizona, and Hawaii were added. Miller Brewing sponsored eighteen events and Cuervo sponsored seven.

Beach volleyball competitions have attracted many sponsors, making professional volleyball a lucrative and dynamic sport.

A Lucrative Tour

By 1983 the number of beach volleyball players was growing, both in the United States and around the world. Some U.S. players decided to form a professional association exclusively for their sport. In July of that year, top players organized as the Association of Volleyball Professionals (AVP). Their stated goal was "to maximize the sport while protecting the commercial interests and integrity of the players."[29] They intended to take an active role in running the tour themselves.

The popularity of beach volleyball matches attracted new commercial sponsors, such as Bollé sunglasses, and in 1986 the total cash prizes on the tour reached $275,000. The game attracted even more fans after cable television began covering AVP matches in 1986 and ABC TV's *Wide World of Sports* covered a beach volleyball match for the first time. During the next decade, more beach events were televised; in both 1991 and '94, ten events appeared on NBC TV. Outside the United States, opportunities to compete were also increasing. In

Australia, for example, a Pro Beach Circuit was formed in 1986.

The AVP continued to build up the sport. By 1988 cash prizes were being offered at twenty-eight tournaments, and Miller Brewing signed an agreement to fund $4.5 million in prizes over the next three years; in turn, the AVP agreed to produce twenty-three Lite Beer beach volleyball events. Cuervo continued as a sponsor, providing $100,000 for three events that year. The AVP began to sponsor the King of the Beach event in 1991. That year about six hundred thousand fans attended beach volleyball tournaments, and the total prize money reached $3.7 million. New sponsors—Evian bottled water and Nestea—came on board in 1994, and prize money reached a new high of $4 million. Players could compete in twenty-seven events, a number that rose to twenty-nine in 1995.

Although most tournaments were organized for men, more women were also becoming involved in beach volleyball, and they formed the Women's Professional Volleyball Association (WPVA) in 1986. As more women around the world took up the sport, the FIVB also began to sponsor tournaments, and the first FIVB women's pro beach volleyball event was held in August

THE DYNAMIC DODDS

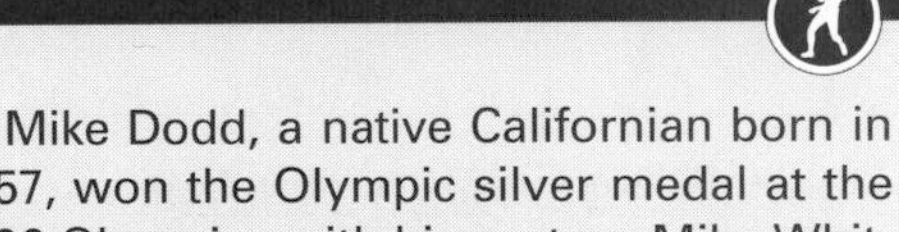

Married since 1986, beach volleyball players Patty Orozco Dodd and Mike Dodd are the only couple to win open titles on the same weekend, a feat they achieved four times in just one year, in 1989.

Born in 1963 in Bogotá, Colombia, Patty Orozco was a star on both her high school basketball and volleyball teams and was rated top high school women's player in the country. At UCLA she lettered in volleyball four years, was an All-American twice, and played on the Bruins' 1984 NCAA Division I women's championship team. She also played on a MLV championship team, the Los Angeles Starlites, in 1987 and '88. As of 2000 Patty Dodd had competed in 90 events, including 17 grand slam events, and had played with 19 partners. She had 45 final-four finishes, including 12 firsts, 8 seconds, 11 thirds, and 14 fourths.

Mike Dodd, a native Californian born in 1957, won the Olympic silver medal at the 1996 Olympics with his partner Mike Whitmarsh. That year he was also named the AVP Most Inspirational Player, Best Defensive Player, and Sportsman of the Year. For several years he and Whitmarsh compiled an impressive record, winning 7 open titles in 1995, with 9 second-place and 5 third-place finishes that same year, and 3 open wins in 1994, along with 9 second-place finishes and 5 third-place finishes.

Dodd began playing beach volleyball at age ten when he and his brother Ted paired up for amateur events. Dodd made history at age sixteen when he became the youngest player ever to earn an AAA ranking (which allows a player to compete in the highest level of play in beach volleyball competition). He earned his first career victory at the 1981 State Beach event with Tim Hovland.

1992 in Almería, Spain. A FIVB world championship series for women players was launched the next year. In addition to women's and men's teams, some tournaments are coed events for teams of one man and one woman.

International Competition

By the 1970s beach volleyball was taken seriously as a competitive international sport. Big-name sponsors and media coverage brought more attention to the game, increasing the number of fans and inspiring more young players to pursue the sport. Large tournaments drew players from around the world.

By 1986 beach volleyball had grown so popular that an international exhibition in Rio de Janiero, Brazil, drew five thousand fans, and beach volleyball was officially recognized by the FIVB. The first FIVB men's beach volleyball World Championships were played in February 1987 in Ipanema, Brazil, and that year the AVP tour expanded to include events in nine states and four countries. The FIVB also promoted the World Beach Series, the Indoor World League, and the European Grand Prix tournaments. The Pro Beach Circuit was also founded in Australia.

During the late 1990s the AVP experienced some financial problems, and players decided it was too time-consuming to manage the large, complex organization that the AVP had become. The organization was restructured in 1999 and again in 2001. Professional management began to take a larger role in managing the tour. AVP executives regarded the 2000 tour as a success, and they planned a schedule of twelve events, including the King of the Beach tournament, for 2001. Sponsors—including Sunkist, Paul Mitchell, and Wilson Sporting Goods—had committed more than $1 million for the season. Mike Whitmarsh, player and Olympic medalist, said, "We want to get back to 20 events a year with prize money at $3 million."[30]

In addition to the AVP tour, a new pro league for men, the Beach Volleyball America (BVA) Tour, was launched in 2001. It scheduled eight tournaments with prizes totaling $450,000 for the year. During its first year, 2000, the BVA had sponsored only women's tournaments. The 2000 Olympic gold medalists, Eric Fonoimoana and Dain Blanton, joined the BVA tour, which counted Speedo, Mikasa, and Outpost.com among its sponsors. The BVA played by international rules, which differ from those used in the AVP tour. They feature smaller courts, a larger ball, and rally-scoring rules, all of which tend to speed up play. The FIVB, which oversees the international game, has endorsed the BVA as the official national tour for U.S. men's and women's teams.

Women's professional beach volleyball has experienced more difficulties than the men's tour. In 1998, for example, the wom-

Jacqui Silva of Brazil is considered one of the best setters in the game. She and teammate Sandra Pires won the first Olympic medals ever by Brazilian women.

en's beach volleyball and four-person beach volleyball tours were canceled because of financial and organizational problems. However, both men and women finally were able to compete for Olympic medals beginning in 1996.

Olympic Status

Beach volleyball players worked for years to make their sport part of the Summer Olympics. In 1993 the International Olympic Committee (IOC) agreed to grant two-person beach volleyball provisional status

A MODEL PLAYER: GABRIELLE "GABBY" REECE

One of the best-known volleyball players and a spokesperson for her sport, Gabrielle Reece was born in the Virgin Islands in 1970. At Florida State University, the six feet three Reece set school season records for both solo and total blocks, and she was inducted into the state's athletic hall of fame. In 1990 she was named the nation's Most Inspiring Collegiate Athlete. While in college she also began a career as a professional model and has appeared on numerous magazine covers.

For five seasons Reece competed in the four-on-four beach volleyball tour and was named Offensive Player of the Year during two of those seasons, 1994 and '95. She also led the league in blocks in 1993 and led four times in kills (1993, '94, '95, '96). During those years her team took first place seven times. In 1999 Reece switched from four-person team play to doubles play after the four-on-four tour was dissolved. She wrote about the challenges of changing her game in an article called "Learning Curves" for the July 1999 issue of *Women's Sports & Fitness*. "The games are quite different. Four-on-four is faster-paced, and each athlete specializes in a certain position. I was a middle blocker; I did a lot of hitting, blocking, and spiking, but very little passing, setting, or defense. I had to learn half of the game. With just two people on a team, a player has to do it all."

Although she was new to the two-person version of the sport, Reece and her partner Holly McPeak took third place at both the Virginia Beach and Chicago tournaments in 1999. She also played in various tournaments with Linda Hanley and Wendy Stammer.

Reece, who has hosted *MTV Sports,* writes a regular column for *Women's Sports & Fitness* magazine and cowrote a book with Karen Karbo called *Big Girl in the Middle* about her life on the pro beach circuit.

and allow both men and women players to compete for medals at the next Olympics.

Twenty-four men's teams and sixteen women's teams represented various countries at the 1996 Olympics in Atlanta, Georgia, where they played on human-made beach about twenty miles south of Olympic Stadium. The president of the IOC, Juan Antonio Samaranch, presented the medals, another sign that the sport had achieved real recognition.

In the women's finals, two Brazilian women's teams captured the gold and silver medals. The gold medalists were twenty-three-year-old Sandra Pires and thirty-four-year-old Jacqueline (Jacqui) Silva, who has been called one of the best setters in the game. Silva had competed twice before at the Olympics in indoor volleyball. In the final match, Pires and Silva defeated their opponents, Monica Rodrigues and Adriana Ramos Samuel, 12–11 and 12–6. These were the first Olympic medals ever won by Brazilian women.

That year, Australia also scored a first, winning its first volleyball medal ever when the team of Kerri Pottharst and Nathalie Cook won the bronze in the women's beach volleyball event. At the 2000 Olympics, the duo defeated Adriana Behar and Shelda Bede of Brazil in two sets to capture the gold before an enthusiastic crowd of fellow Australians at Bondi Beach Centre Court. Although Cook and Pottharst had played the Brazilian team nineteen times, this was only the fifth time they had defeated them, and the gold medal was their second international title in beach volleyball after playing in forty-one FIVB Beach Volleyball World Tour events.

Although several U.S. women's teams had won international competitions, they did not win any Olympic medals in beach volleyball in either 1996 or 2000. In Atlanta the U.S. team of Barbra Fontana and Linda Hanley finished fourth, while Holly McPeak and Nancy Reno placed fifth. In the 2000 Sydney games, the two-women teams of Annett Davis and Jenny Johnson Jordan and Misty May and Holly McPeak were both defeated in their quarterfinal matches, losing to Japan and Brazil.

The Brazilians had dominated many international competitions on the beach circuit throughout the late 1990s, and they won three medals at the 2000 Olympics: the men's silver and the women's silver and bronze. Capturing the silver were Adriana Behar and Shelda Bede, while Adriana Samuel and Sandra Pires took the bronze.

A triumphant United States took home two consecutive gold medals in the men's competition. U.S. teams won gold and silver medals in 1996 when beach volleyball legends Karch Kiraly and Kent Steffes defeated Mike Dodd and Mike Whitmarsh in the finals with scores of 12–5 and 12–8. After the match Whitmarsh said, "I'm very happy for Karch and Kent. They've been the dominant team for four or five years. If you lose, you want to lose to the best. Besides, Karch Kiraly has done more for volleyball than anyone else."[31]

A Canadian team, Mark Heese and John Child, won the bronze. Heese, age thirty-one, and Child, thirty-three, had been playing together for six years and were known

Canadian Mark Heese and his teammate, John Child, are renowned for their powerful dives and incredible returns.

for making incredible digs, diving low to return powerful serves. In an interview, Heese said, "Scrappy is the word I like to use. Those big guys can come in with as hard a hit as possible and nothing makes us happier than to somehow get it up and squeak it back over to their side."[32]

Twenty-four men's teams competed at the 2000 Sydney Olympics, where the American team of Dain Blanton and Eric Fonoimoana, both Californians, won the gold medal in an upset victory over the Brazilian team of José Marco Melo and Ricardo Santos. After the match a delighted Blanton said, "The only way we played that well was to play against a team that good."[33] The event was extremely popular, and the men played to sell-out crowds of about twenty thousand people a day.

A Bright Future

The game of beach volleyball continues to gain new fans and players, with more tournaments each year, new sponsors, and the addition of the Beach Volleyball Association (BVA) circuit.

Inspired by an increasing number of beach volleyball events on television and in the Olympics, more young people are also taking up the sport. The AVP has responded by organizing more junior beach volleyball tournaments for up-and-coming players. In 2000 the AVP/BVA hosted a tour that included eight stops at various California beach locations, to coincide with the AVP tour.

Beach volleyball was a provisional Olympic sport during the 1996 and 2000 games, but in 2001 the IOC decided to make it a permanent event, beginning with the 2004 games. With more cable sports stations, fans will probably see an increasing number of tournaments on television, in addition to Olympic coverage. This kind of exposure has brought more recognition to both indoor and beach volleyball players. Many fans now recognize top players by name and by their distinctive playing styles and personalities.

All-Time Greats

Volleyball is a team sport, and some teams have achieved enormous success, even legendary status, through the years. Certain individual players have also become stars, playing a key role in their team's success. In addition, some players and coaches have contributed new techniques to the game. Talented volleyball teams and athletes come from countries around the world.

Kamikaze Volleyball

In 1964 fans were dazzled by a group of athletes who took the game to new heights—sometimes by diving for the ball. They were the Japanese women's team, dubbed the "Wizards" or "Whiz Girls of the Orient" after they won that year's Olympics, held in Tokyo. Many Japanese families bought their first television sets just before the games so they could watch the action at home.

Years of hard work and intense coaching produced the team's gold-medal performance. Coach Hirofumi Daimatsu required his team to train seven days a week for at least six hours a day with only one week off during the year. Daimatsu's methods were strict and even harsh, as he badgered the players and insulted them when he did not like their performance. Sportswriter Bud Greenspan says, "Training sessions under Daimatsu were brutal mentally and physically. Practices consisted of continuous dives, rolls and tumbles. The sessions were designed to shatter, then rebuild, the spirit of the women."[34]

DEBBIE GREEN: THE YOUNGEST ALL-AMERICAN

Called one of the greatest setters in volleyball history, Debbie Green became volleyball's youngest All-American when she was only sixteen years old. Green, who was born in South Korea, was told she would never rise to the top in the sport because of her height—5-feet 4 inches. However, she continued to practice and improve her weakest point, her serve, and became a top collegiate player at the University of Southern California. In 1975 she was named an All-American.

As part of the U.S. women's national team, Green played in the 1979 Pan American Games, where her team came in fourth, and also on the bronze-winning U.S. team at the 1982 World Championships. Two years later Green and her teammates triumphed to earn a silver medal at the 1984 Olympics.

Debbie Green was inducted into the Volleyball Hall of Fame in 1995.

Besides perfecting the basic moves of the game, these women were incredibly agile and fast. Observers called their game style "Kamikaze volleyball," named after the Japanese airmen who were trained to crash their planes during World War II missions. After their 1964 victory, team captain Masae Kasai said, "Even though we had been through so much pain and anguish, it was all worth it."[35] The Japanese women repeated their triumphant performance at the 1976 Olympics. Their playing style had a vast influence on the game as athletes around the world tried similar moves and took the game to a new level.

In December 2000 the FIVB named the Japanese team of 1960–65 the greatest women's team of the twentieth century "for the team's endurance, top level performances, fighting spirit shown to the crowds and world wide popularity . . . making Volleyball a symbol of women's achievement in sports."[36]

"You Love to Watch Them Play": The Cuban Women's Team

No discussion of great teams could overlook the Cuban women's national team that dominated international competition in the 1990s and won three consecutive gold medals in 1992, '96, and 2000, a feat that has never been duplicated. The Cuban women also won four consecutive World Cups and the 1994 and 1998 World Championships. In August 2000 the women, known as "Las Morenas del Caribe" (the dark women of the Caribbean), achieved a grand slam by also winning the Grand Prix in Manila, Philippines.

What accounts for their phenomenal record? Athletes in Cuba begin training at an early age, once their aptitude becomes evident, and the government strongly supports its national teams. The Cuban women, who are among the tallest women's volleyball players in the world, are trained to play a power game, jumping high and hitting hard. In training they often use a net the same height as male players use: 2.43 meters, nineteen centimeters higher than the one used in women's games. Along with their talent and strength, the Cuban women work extremely well together and show great tenacity in a match. Says 2000 Team USA volleyball coach Mick Haley, "They are the best. You love to watch them play. You don't like to play against them."[37]

A Versatile Star: Karcsi (Karch) Kiraly

In Hungary, where his father was born, the name Kiraly means "king," and Karch Kiraly has "ruled" in both beach and indoor volleyball. By the end of 1999, Kiraly had a record 141 AVP titles in pro beach volleyball and topped the earnings list at $2,844,065 in April 2000. He has won all the big titles, including the World Cup, Pan American Games, Savin Cup, World Championships, and Olympic gold medals for both indoor and beach volleyball.

Karch Kiraly, right, and Kent Steffes accept the 1996 Olympic gold in Atlanta.

Born in Michigan in 1960, Kiraly grew up in California. He enjoyed playing volleyball on local beaches and entered his first tournament at age eleven, playing with his father, a former volleyball champion who taught him to play.

Kiraly played on the varsity indoor volleyball team at UCLA, where he studied biochemistry. During his years on the team as a setter/hitter, UCLA captured three U.S. collegiate championships. Kiraly was one of the first players to promote the jump serve, and fans have also enjoyed watching him toss the ball with one hand while holding his other hand on his hip, a move that has become his trademark.

In 1982 he became part of the U.S. men's volleyball team. At age twenty-three, he was the youngest player when the team won both the Olympic gold medal in 1984 and the men's World Championships in 1986. Kiraly played in all nineteen games at the Olympics, more than any other player, and commentators praised his outstanding defensive moves and lethal spike shot.

Although he received tempting offers to move abroad and play for other teams, Kiraly remained with the U.S. team and helped it to earn another gold medal at the 1988 Olympics, where he was voted team MVP. During the '80s he was also named MVP at the World Cup tournament (1985) and World's Best Volleyball Player (1986) by FIVB president Ruben Acosta. In 1991 he was again named MVP, as well as best digger, this time at the Club World Championships.

From 1988 to 1991, Kiraly played on a pro team in Italy before embarking on a professional career on the beach volleyball circuit. He immediately dominated the tour, winning the King of the Beach title in 1991, '92, '93, and '96. Five times—in 1990, '92, '93, '94, and '95—Kiraly was voted the AVP's Most Valuable Player.

When beach volleyball debuted at the Olympics in 1996, Kiraly and his then-partner Kent Steffes defeated teams from around the world to capture the gold medal. This made Kiraly the first man in history to win three gold medals in the sport of volleyball. A shoulder injury sidelined Kiraly in 1997, but he worked to come back and qualified for the 2000 Olympics.

In December 2000 the FIVB named Karch Kiraly Best Volleyball Player of the Twentieth Century—Men. USA Volleyball executive director Kerry Klostermann said, "There is no athlete representing the sport of volleyball that is more deserving of this honor. Karch is in a class by himself and it has been our extreme privilege to have him represent USA Volleyball and the United States over the past two decades."[38]

Woman Player of the Century: Regla Torres (Herrera)

During the 1990s Cuba's Regla Torres was often called the best woman player in the

"Best woman volleyball player in the world" was often used to describe Cuba's Regla Torres in the 1990s.

world. In 2000 the FIVB made this title official when it named her best women's volleyball player of the twentieth century. The six feet two athlete is a particularly effective blocker, known for her ability to shut down power hitters, but she also excels as a server, hitter, and receiver. Born in 1975 in Havana, Torres began playing club volleyball in 1983. At age sixteen she earned a coveted spot on the Cuban national women's team. Torres was only seventeen when she captured her first Olympic medal in 1992, making her the youngest woman ever to win an Olympic gold medal in volleyball.

During the 1990s Torres and her teammates impressed the volleyball world in one event after another. The team won three silver medals at the Grand Prix event (1994, '96, and '97), as well as a bronze (1995) and two golds, in 1993 and 2000, and a World Cup gold medal in 1995. Torres continued to receive special awards for her varied achievements on the court, including being named best receiver (World Grand Champions Cup, 1993) and best blocker (World Championships, 1994 and '98, and World Grand Prix, '97). In the 1998 tournament, she managed forty-two successful blocks and also scored more points than any other player. In 1993, when her team won the World Grand Prix gold medal, Torres was named best server; she was named best server again in 1998 at the BCV Volley Masters tournament. At the 1998 World Championships, Torres was named best player as well as best blocker, and she repeated both feats at the 1999 World Championships.

At the 2000 Olympics in Sydney, Australia, she was voted best spiker, but once again commentators noticed how her blocking ability helped the team win. During a tough quarterfinals match against Croatia, the team faced Barbara Jelic, a strong hitter. However, as one sportswriter pointed out,

"Torres was in the Croatian's face the entire contest, allowing Jelic just 17 kills and a paltry four in the opening set."[39]

Although Cuba is a communist nation where athletes are regarded as government employees, Cuban officials have permitted Torres to play pro volleyball in Italy for the Modena league and to keep some of the money she earns through playing and awards. She continues to play with the Cuban team for important events.

The "Iron Hammer": Lang Ping

Nicknamed the "Iron Hammer," Lang Ping is perhaps the most famous female volleyball player in Chinese history as well as a respected coach. She was known for her quick moves on the court and relentless attacks. During her career she was named best player in China six times, best player in Asia five times, and best player in the world four times.

THE VOLLEYBALL HALL OF FAME

Located in the town where William G. Morgan invented volleyball, the Hall of Fame began as an idea in 1971 when the Greater Holyoke Chamber of Commerce organized a committee to develop a place to display volleyball memorabilia and to honor people who have achieved greatness in the sport. The U.S. Volleyball Association decided to place items related to volleyball history in the local public library until a place could be erected. In 1985 William G. Morgan was inducted as the Hall of Fame's first member, and space was set aside in a local building the next year for the hall. It was opened to the public in June 1987. The hall has since been located in various buildings while awaiting a permanent home in Holyoke. Besides players, Hall of Fame inductees include outstanding coaches, officials, and leaders in the game. All must have contributed at least seven years of outstanding service to the sport in his or her particular field. Players and coaches must also have been retired for five years.

The Volleyball Hall of Fame in Holyoke, Massachusetts, displays plaques of inductees, photographs, and a half-sized volleyball court with wooden cutouts of all six court positions.

The hall, which contains historical memorabilia, papers, and awards, also sponsors special events, including the Spalding Volleyball Hall of Fame Morgan classic tournament for top collegiate teams, as well as teaching clinics.

Born in 1960, Lang Ping grew up in Beijing, where she enjoyed several sports. She later said, "I ran track, high-jumped and played soccer. But since I was very tall, I was always told to play basketball."[40] Because she was so thin—five feet eleven inches and just over a hundred pounds—her basketball coaches decided that the sport was too rough for her and sent her to another gymnasium to play volleyball. From the start she excelled and became the top player of the team and of the entire Beijing City League. Lang Ping was also an outstanding jumper who could soar thirty-five inches above the court.

Ping played on the Chinese national team from 1978 to 1985. During those years they won second place in the 1978 Asian Games, and in 1981 they finally defeated the Japanese women's team to win the World Cup in Tokyo, then won their first World Championship title in 1982. She recalls that her team practiced eight hours a day, six days a week, for six months before winning their gold medal at the 1984 Summer Olympics in Los Angeles. The Chinese government let people stay home from work to watch the match live, and it was said to be the most-watched event on TV in Chinese history. A national holiday was declared after the team won. The next year the team won another World Cup. In all, Lang Ping competed in 215 tournaments.

Ping then joined the Italian professional volleyball league, and her team won the Italian Championships in both 1989 and '90. With a B.A. degree from the Beijing Institute of Physical Education, she pursued her master's degree in sports administration at the University of New Mexico, where she lived in 1986 and '87. Ping then served as assistant coach for the New Mexico Lobos in 1987 and from 1991–95. She also played for the Chinese women's team during part of 1990. Continuing her coaching career, she guided the Chinese women's national team from 1995 to 1998, and it captured a gold medal at the World Championships and in the Asian Games in 1996. In 2000 the FIVB gave Ping a special award as one of the three best women volleyball players of the twentieth century.

Flo Hyman

Although she had been too shy to try out for her high school volleyball team as a fourteen-year-old in Inglewood, California, Flo Hyman became a legendary spiker and one of the best players in the world. At six feet five inches, she towered over many of her teammates and competitors, and she perfected a slow one-two takeoff that gave her forward motion as she rose to hit the ball. Sports historian Sue Macy writes, "More than any other U.S. athlete, Flora 'Flo' Hyman put women's volleyball on the map."[41]

In 1974 Hyman was chosen as one of the players who would form a women's team training specifically for the Olympics and hopefully going on to win a medal at the

Flo Hyman, 6'5" member of the 1984 Olympic silver medal team died suddenly at the age of 31 during a match in Japan. In her honor the Women's Sports Foundation created the Flo Hyman Award, given each year to an outstanding female athlete.

1980 games. The players left their jobs and moved to a training center in California where they worked with top coach Arie Selinger.

The team did not qualify for the 1976 Olympics, but their hard work paid off when they qualified for the 1980 games in Moscow. However, the United States boycotted those Olympics for political reasons. Hyman and her six teammates continued to train hard, eight hours a day and six days a week, now setting their sights on the 1984 games, to be held in Los Angeles. In the meantime, in 1981 Hyman was named best female hitter in the world.

In an exciting final match at the 1984 games, the Chinese women's team won the gold medal while the U.S. women's team won the silver. Hyman called it one of the proudest moments in her life, saying, "We accomplished a lot. We're proud of our silver medal."[42] She then decided to play for a Japanese team, since volleyball players had professional leagues in that country.

In 1986 Flo Hyman died suddenly at age thirty-one during a match in Japan. It was discovered that she had a rare genetic disease, Marfan's syndrome, that she had not even known about. In her honor, the Women's Sports Foundation created the Flo Hyman Memorial Award, given each year to "an outstanding female athlete who exemplifies the same dignity, spirit, and commitment to excellence" as Flo Hyman.

Beach Legend: Sinjin (Christopher St. John) Smith

Regarded as one of the hardest-working, most-talented beach volleyball players in history, Smith was born in Santa Monica, California, in 1957 and played his first beach volleyball tournament in 1977 with future volleyball Hall-of-Famer Ron Von Hagen. Later that year he won his first career match, playing with Mike Norman. At UCLA Smith earned All-American honors twice and helped his team win two national indoor volleyball championships. From 1979–82 Smith was also a member of the U.S. national men's volleyball team.

For ten years on the beach circuit, Smith paired with Randy Stoklos, and they won a record-setting 113 matches, including two coveted Manhattan Beach Open titles and three U.S. Open Championships. During the 1980s and '90s, Smith and Stoklos were regarded as the top team on the AVP tour. Smith won two more Manhattan Beach Open titles playing with Jim Menges in 1979 and with Karch Kiraly in 1980, as well as two more U.S. Championships with Kiraly. In 1992 he became the second player to reach the $1 million mark in prizes.

Starting in the mid-1990s, Smith left the AVP to play in the FIVB Beach Volleyball World Tour. Smith strongly supported making beach volleyball an Olympic sport and qualified for the 1996 games. Although he was nearly forty, making him one of the older players, Smith and partner Carl Henkel finished fifth. Some sports historians consider their match against Kiraly and Kent Steffes, the eventual gold medalists, the best beach volleyball match ever played.

Smith continued to play in some tournaments until August 2001, when he announced he would retire after the Manhattan Beach Open. By the end of his career, he had won 139 beach titles, second only to Karch Kiraly.

Beach Gold: Kent Steffes

With partner Karch Kiraly, Kent Steffes made history in 1996 by winning the first Olympic gold medal in the sport of beach volleyball. Born in 1968 in Pacific Palisades, California, Steffes grew up playing the sport. He won the title of 1986 National High School Player of the Year and was rated as the nation's top amateur player when he attended Stanford University. In his second year, he transferred to UCLA but stopped playing college volleyball in 1988 to begin playing full-time as a pro. Steffes also continued his education and in 1993 received a degree in economics from UCLA.

Just one year into the pro tour, Steffes won his first tournament at Seal Beach, playing with Jon Stevenson. He achieved eight open wins in 1991, when he became the first AVP player to win with three different partners in the same year. The next year, with eighteen more wins to his credit, twenty-four-year-old Steffes became the youngest player to be ranked number one by the AVP. During 1992 he played most often with Karch Kiraly, and together they won thirteen consecutive tournaments. Sportswriter Franz Lidz, who praised Steffes as a great blocker and a great digger, wrote, "Steffes sizzles across the sand."[43] The next year Steffes and Kiraly won eighteen more opens together, including all five of the major tournaments on the AVP tour. Steffes's earnings had reached $1 million in just five years on the tour.

Continuing to play with Kiraly, Steffes won seventeen of twenty-two tournaments that he entered in 1994 and four in 1995, although a shoulder injury sidelined him during much of that season. However, he recovered in time to take the gold medal when beach volleyball debuted at the 1996 Olympics.

Beginning in 1997 Steffes played most often with José Loiola. As of 1998 he had achieved 102 first-place finishes in AVP matches and ranked second on the prize list, with a total of nearly $2.5 million, placing him second on the all-time earning list.

Flyin' Liz Masakayan

Born in 1964 in Quezon City, Philippines, Liz Masakayan grew up in Santa Monica, California, where she excelled both as a student and an athlete. Masakayan later said, "I played little league baseball with the boys all the way through senior league. I made the all-star team when I was fourteen. The beach was half a mile away so I played beach volleyball all the time, and I also played soccer on all-boy teams."[44] Masakayan said she learned valuable lessons about hard work and teamwork as a child. Her father died when she was ten, so she and her three older siblings did the household chores while her mother worked to support the family.

At UCLA Masakayan was one of the greatest women players in the school's history and earned the nickname the "Flyin' Masakayan." During her years as a Bruin, the team won the 1984 NCAA title and Masakayan was an All-American, as well as a two-time winner of the American Volleyball Coaches Association (AVCA) award. She was part of the 1988 U.S. team that won the silver medal at the NORCECA championships held in Cuba in 1988.

Moving into international beach competition, Masakayan played her first FIVB event with Linda Chisholm in 1992 in Rio de Janeiro, Brazil. She then paired with Karolyn Kirby, and they dominated the women's pro tour from 1993–95, winning twenty-six titles, including thirteen consecutive events. They reached fifteen FIVB tour semifinals and won three event titles. Masakayan was named MVP on the tour in 1992, and she and Kirby were named co-MVPs in 1993. The next year the pair won the gold medal at the Goodwill Games as well as the FIVB Beach Volleyball World Tour title. However, in 1995 Masakayan suffered a knee injury at a tournament and had to take time off.

Liz Masakayan, nicknamed "the Flyin' Masakayan" during her years at UCLA, is one of the most outstanding athletes now playing on the beach volleyball circuit.

From 1990–93 Masakayan worked at UCLA as an assistant coach. One of the players she coached, Elaine Youngs, has often been her beach volleyball partner since 1997, and the pair won two tournaments in 1998. Throughout 1999 they won numerous titles in U.S. events. As of 2000 Masakayan had played in forty-two international competitions and had finished in the top ten in all of them except three. That year she and Youngs captured their first international title at the Brazil Open tournament and won titles in China and Portugal.

"Big Red": Steve Timmons

With three Olympic medals in volleyball and an array of other awards, it was no surprise that Steve Timmons was inducted into the Volleyball Hall of Fame in 1998. A powerful player who hit strongly from the back or the front row, Timmons also became known to fans for his lively personality and red flat-top haircut.

Six feet five Timmons, who has excelled both indoors and on the beach, was born in 1958 in Newport Beach, California. At the University of Southern California, he played on their 1980 NCAA Championship teams and was an All-American in 1980 and 1981. Timmons went on to win two World Championships and a World Cup medal, as well as his Olympic medals—gold in 1984 and '88 and bronze in '92. At the 1984 Olympics, Timmons made a team-high of 106 kills in 184 attempts and was named MVP of the Olympics. He was also all-tournament at the USA Cup and MVP of the World Super Four Tournament, held in Japan.

After quitting the U.S. men's team in 1989 to play in the Italian pro league Il Messaggero, Timmons helped that team win the league championship. In 1991 Timmons returned to the U.S. men's team to help them rebuild and compete at the Barcelona Olympics. Timmons's experience and hitting skills helped the team to win third place at the games.

During the 1997 season, Timmons rejoined the Italian pro league to play again for Il Messaggero. Timmons is proud of his role in promoting volleyball. He says, "It was a sport that people thought of as a game to play until the hamburgers were done at the park, and we helped expose people to how explosive and exciting six-man, indoor volleyball can be."[45]

Volleyball Moves into Its Second Century

In 1995 people around the world celebrated the hundredth anniversary of volleyball with tournaments, awards ceremonies, and special stamp issues. Volleyball's first hundred years had been marked by changing rules and techniques for playing the game, as well as tremendous growth. Volleyball had moved out of a small-town YMCA to become a leading amateur and competitive sport. Yet the game retained the versatility and flexibility that had sparked its initial success in the 1890s as a fun game for amateur players.

Statistics show that more people are playing volleyball than ever before. According to the National Federation of State High School Associations, in 2000 more than 400,000 girls competed in volleyball at more than 12,400 schools. The NCAA reported that 784 institutions sponsored women's volleyball for more than 10,300 student athletes in 1992; by 1995 there were twelve hundred women's college teams and sixty collegiate volleyball teams for men. USVBA reached nearly 100,000 members in the late 1990s. Other volleyball organizations were growing as well. As of 1998 the FIVB had 217 affiliate federations.

In the United States, between three hundred to four hundred people were professional volleyball players. They competed in events organized by the National Volleyball Association (NVA), Fédération Internationale de Volleyball (FIVB), Association of Volleyball Professionals (AVP), American Volleyball League (AVL), and National

Volleyball League (NVL). The United States Professional Volleyball League (USPV) was also formed to promote opportunities for top women players. Its 2001 USPV Dream Tour, featuring a twelve-member team of top women players, played matches in the United States and other countries, including Holland and the Dominican Republic.

Volleyball continues to appeal to all ages and different types of players. The Junior Olympics, for ages ten to eighteen, attracted forty-eight thousand young players during the 1990s. Senior citizens have been playing the game in increasing numbers, too. To adapt volleyball to seniors' special needs, physical education experts suggest they play with nine players per side, rather than six, and vary the height of the net, depending on the skill level of the group. They may also decide to let the server choose a position closer to the net and use a ball slightly lighter than regulation. More time-outs can also be taken, as needed. These adaptations are also used for people with disabilities.

As was true throughout history, the rules for volleyball have continued to evolve. Some major changes occurred in the late 1990s when new rules for international competitions were introduced to make the sport even more exciting. The FIVB announced that it would switch to rally scoring, meaning that every error would become a point for the other team. Now a team could score on any point, whether or not it served the ball on that point. To go along with this quicker method of scoring, the number of points per game was increased to twenty-five instead of fifteen for the first four sets and fifteen for the final set. Matches are still the best-of-five sets, and each set must be won by a margin of two points.

Another change involved the option to use an additional player called a "libero," who wears a different jersey from the rest of the team and plays solely in the back row. A libero may substitute for any player an unlimited number of times in order to strengthen the defensive play of the team but does not serve, spike, or rotate to the front row. Using the libero helps to sustain rallies in the men's game, where in the past strong offensive play by either team could end points quickly.

Other new rules affected players' clothing. In 1998 the FIVB banned long-sleeved shirts and said uniforms could not be loose or baggy. Instead, they must follow the lines of the body, with women having the option to wear either a one-piece or two-piece outfit. A player's number must appear on the right leg of the shorts, with the country flag and name on the left front of the shirt. Last names go on the back of the shirt above the player's number. The new scoring system, use of the libero, and new dress code debuted at the 2000 Olympics in Sydney.

The libero dives for the ball while teammates look on.

Since 2000 other organizations have announced rule changes in line with the FIVB. In 2001 the National Association for Girls and Women in Sport (NAGWS), which makes rules for NCAA and National Association of Intercollegiate Athletics (NAIA) women's volleyball, decided to use the rally-scoring format with games one through four going to thirty points and to fifteen in the fifth and deciding game.

Based on its history, volleyball will probably continue to evolve and attract new players and fans. According to Hall of Fame coach Arie Selinger:

> Volleyball has changed tremendously, not only in rules, techniques, and concepts, but also in the physical abilities of the players. Perhaps more than any other sport, power volleyball allows expression of the athlete's fullest capabilities. There is no reason to believe that the future will hold any less change and development.[46]

Awards and Statistics

Olympic Games

Men

Year	Gold	Silver	Bronze
1964	Soviet Union (USSR)	Czechoslovakia	Japan
1968	Soviet Union (USSR)	Japan	Czechoslovakia
1972	Japan	East Germany (GDR)	Soviet Union (USSR)
1976	Poland	Soviet Union (USSR)	Cuba
1980	Soviet Union (USSR)	Bulgaria	Italy
1984	United States	Brazil	Italy
1988	United States	Soviet Union (USSR)	Argentina
1992	Brazil	Netherlands (Holland)	United States
1996	Netherlands (Holland)	Italy	Yugoslavia
2000	Yugoslavia	Russia	Italy

Statistics

Medal Table

Country	Gold	Silver	Bronze	Total
Soviet Union (USSR)	3	2	1	6
United States	2	-	1	3
Japan	1	1	1	3
Italy	-	1	2	3
Brazil	1	1	-	2
Netherlands	1	1	-	2
Yugoslavia	1	-	1	2
Czechoslovakia	-	1	1	2

Players with Three or More Olympic Medals

Player	Gold	Silver	Bronze	Total
Yuri Poyarkov, URS	'64, '68		'72	3
Stephen Timmons, USA	'84, '88		'92	3
Vyacheslav Zaitsev, URS	'80	'76, '88		3
Katsutoshi Nekoda, JPN	'72	'68	'64	3
Masayuki Minami, JPN	'72	'68	'64	3
Vladimir Kondra, URS	'80	'76	'72	3

Olympic Games

Women

Year	Gold	Silver	Bronze
1964	Japan	Soviet Union (USSR)	Poland
1968	Soviet Union (USSR)	Japan	Poland
1972	Soviet Union (USSR)	Japan	North Korea
1976	Japan	Soviet Union (USSR)	South Korea
1980	Soviet Union (USSR)	East Germany (GDR)	Bulgaria
1984	China	United States	Japan
1988	Soviet Union (USSR)	Peru	China
1992	Cuba	Soviet Union (Unified Team)	United States
1996	Cuba	China	Brazil
2000	Cuba	Russia	Brazil

Statistics

Medal Table

Country	Gold	Silver	Bronze	Total
Soviet Union (USSR + UNT)	4	3	-	7
Japan	2	2	1	5
Cuba	3	-	-	3
China	1	1	1	3
United States	-	1	1	2
Poland	-	-	2	2
Brazil	-	-	2	2

Players with Three or More Olympic Medals

Player	Gold	Silver	Bronze	Total
Inna Ryskal, URS	'68, '72	'64, '76		4
Regla Bell, CUB	'92, '96, '00			3
Marleny Costa, CUB	'92, '96, '00			3
Idalmis Gato, CUB	'92, '96, '00			3
Lilia Izquierdo, CUB	'92, '96, '00			3
Mireya Luis Hernández, CUB	'92, '96, '00			3
Regla Torres, CUB	'92, '96, '00			3
Ljudmila Buldakova, URS	'68, '72	'64		3
Nina Smoleeva, URS	'68, '72	'76		3

Beach Volleyball/Olympic Games

Men

Year	Gold	Silver	Bronze
1996	Karch Kiraly–Kent Steffes, USA	Mike Dodd–Mike Whitmarsh, USA	John Child–Mark Heese, CAN
2000	Dain Blanton–Eric Steffes, USA	José Marco Melo–Ricardo Santos, BRA	Joerg Ahmann–Axel Hager, GER

Women

Year	Gold	Silver	Bronze
1996	Jacqui Silva–Sandra Pires, BRA	Monica Rodrigues–Adriana Samuel, BRA	Nathalie Cook–Kerri Pottharst, AUS
2000	Nathalie Cook–Kerri Pottharst, AUS	Adriana Behar–Shelda Bede, BRA	Sandra Pires–Adriana Samuel, BRA

World Championships

Men

Site	Year	Gold	Silver	Bronze
Prague	1949	Soviet Union (USSR)	Czechoslovakia	Bulgaria
Moscow	1952	Soviet Union (USSR)	Czechoslovakia	Bulgaria
Paris	1956	Czechoslovakia	Romania	Soviet Union (USSR)
Rio de Janeiro	1960	Soviet Union (USSR)	Czechoslovakia	Romania
Moscow	1962	Soviet Union (USSR)	Czechoslovakia	Romania
Prague	1966	Czechoslovakia	Romania	Soviet Union (USSR)
Sofia	1970	East Germany (GDR)	Bulgaria	Japan
Mexico DF	1974	Polonia	Soviet Union (USSR)	Japan
Rome	1978	Soviet Union (USSR)	Italy	Cuba
Buenos Aires	1982	Soviet Union (USSR)	Brazil	Argentina
Paris	1986	United States	Soviet Union (USSR)	Bulgaria
Rio de Janeiro	1990	Italy	Cuba	Soviet Union (USSR)
Athens, GRE	1994	Italy	Netherlands	United States
Osaka	1998	Italy	Yugoslavia	Cuba

Medal Table

Country	Gold	Silver	Bronze	Total
Soviet Union (USSR)	6	2	3	11
Czechoslovakia	2	4	-	6
Italy	3	1	-	4
Romania	-	2	2	4
Bulgaria	-	1	3	4
Cuba	-	1	2	3
United States	1	-	1	2
Japan	-	-	2	2

World Championships

Women

Site	Year	Gold	Silver	Bronze
Moscow	1952	Soviet Union (USSR)	Polonia	Czechoslovakia
Paris	1956	Soviet Union (USSR)	Romania	Polonia
Rio de Janeiro	1960	Soviet Union (USSR)	Japan	Czechoslovakia
Moscow	1962	Japan	Soviet Union (USSR)	Polonia
Tokyo	1967	Japan	United States	South Korea

Site	Year	Gold	Silver	Bronze
Varna, BUL	1970	Soviet Union (USSR)	Japan	South Korea
Guadalajara	1974	Japan	Soviet Union (USSR)	South Korea
Leningrad	1978	Cuba	Japan	Soviet Union (USSR)
Lima	1982	China	Peru	United States
Prague	1986	China	Cuba	Peru
Beijing	1990	Soviet Union (USSR)	China	United States
São Paolo	1994	Cuba	Brazil	Russia
Osaka	1998	Cuba	China	Russia

Medal Table

Country	Gold	Silver	Bronze	Total
Soviet Union (USSR)	5	2	1	8
Japan	3	3	-	6
Cuba	3	1	-	4
China	2	2	-	4
Poland	-	1	2	3
United States	-	1	2	3
South Korea	-	-	3	3
Peru	-	1	1	2

Notes

Chapter 1: A New Team Sport

1. James Naismith, *Basketball: Its Origin and Development*. Lincoln: University of Nebraska Press, 1996, p. 33.
2. Quoted in J. Y. Cameron, "The Original Game of Volley Ball," *Physical Education,* July 1896.
3. Quoted in Robert E. Laveaga, *Volleyball, A Man's Game*. New York: A. S. Barnes, 1933, p. 1.
4. Quoted in the *Association Athletic Handbook—Volleyball 1897,* Official Handbook of the Young Men's Christian Associations of North America online, Volleyball Worldwide. www.volleyball.org/rules/rules_1897.html.
5. Quoted in the *Association Athletic Handbook—Volleyball, 1897.*
6. Quoted in the *Association Athletic Handbook—Volleyball, 1897.*
7. Quoted in the *Association Athletic Handbook—Volleyball, 1897.*
8. Quoted in the *Association Athletic Handbook—Volleyball, 1897.*

Chapter 2: Decades of Growth

9. Steven Boga, *Volleyball*. Mechanicsburg, PA: Stackpole Books, 1997, p. 1.
10. Quoted in Laveaga, *Volleyball,* pp. 23–24.
11. Quoted in Laveaga, *Volleyball,* p. 24.
12. Anna de Koven, "The Athletic Woman," *Good Housekeeping,* August 1912, pp. 151–52.
13. Quoted in Lois Banner, *American Beauty*. New York: Knopf, 1983, p. 156.
14. Quoted in "Lou Henry Hoover." http://hoover.nara.gov/education/louhenrybio.html.
15. Quoted in Deborah Crisfield, *Winning Volleyball for Girls.* New York: Facts on File, 1995, p. 5.
16. *Hygeia Magazine,* "Women and Sports," November 1928, p. 63.
17. "FIVB Mission Statement." www.volleyball.org/fivb/.
18. "FIVB's 100 Year History of Volleyball," Volleyball Hall of Fame. www.volleyball.org/FIVB.htm.
19. Darlene A. Kluka and Peter J. Dunn, *Volleyball.* Boston: McGraw-Hill, 2000, p. 4.

Chapter 3: A Global Competitive Sport

20. Quoted in George Gipe, *The Great American Sports Book.* Garden City, NY: Doubleday, 1978, p. 502.

21. Kluka and Dunn, *Volleyball,* p. 11.
22. Quoted in Bud Greenspan, "My Favorite Olympic Moments," *Sports Illustrated,* June 17, 1996.
23. Title IX, Education Amendments of 1972 (Title 20 U.S.C. Sections 1681–1688). www.dol.gov/dol/oasam/public/regs/statutes/titleix.htm.
24. Arie Selinger with Joan Blount-Ackermann, "Introduction," *Power Volleyball.* New York: St. Martin's, 1986.

Chapter 4: Beach Volleyball

25. Gabrielle Reece, "Learning Curves," *Women's Sports & Fitness*, July 1999, p. 67.
26. Quoted in Christina Lessa, *Stories of Triumph: Women Who Win in Sport and in Life*. New York: Universe, 1998, p. 108.
27. Quoted in Michael Dobie, "The 1996 Atlanta Summer Games/What's New for '96/Beach Volleyball: From Sand to Sand Dollars," *Newsday,* July 14, 1996, p. 23.
28. Quoted in Dobie, "The 1996 Atlanta Summer Games," p. 23.
29. Association of Volleyball Professionals (AVP), "History." www.avptour.com/tour_history.cfm.
30. Quoted in Joshua W. Binder, "Beach Volleyball." www.brntwdmagazine.com/june01/games/games-1.html.
31. Quoted in Michael Farber, "Fun in the Sun," *Sports Illustrated*, August 5, 1996, p. 91.
32. Quoted in "Child and Heese Plan to Dig in on the Beach for Another Olympic Medal," September 4, 2000, FIV Volleyball News from Volleyballstuff.com. http://cnews.tribune.com/news/story/0,1162,newsday-olympics-72540,00.html.
33. Quoted in Lisa Dillman, "Americans Beat Brazil for Volleyball Gold," *Los Angeles Times,* September 26, 2000. www.dainblanton.com/olympics2.htm.

Chapter 5: All-Time Greats

34. Greenspan, "My Favorite Olympic Moments."
35. Greenspan, "My Favorite Olympic Moments."
36. Quoted in "The 20th Century's Volleyball Best," FIVB press release, December 11, 2000. www.fivb.ch/PressArea/Press%20Releases/PR%202000.12.11.html.
37. Quoted in Leora Moldofsky, "Volleyball—the Explosive Cubans Don't Just Want to Win; They're Out to Set a Gold-Medal Record," *Time International,* September 18, 2000, p. 105.
38. Quoted in "USA Volleyball News," December 12, 2000, USA Volleyball News Headlines. www.usavolleyball.org/news/news_121200.htm.
39. Quoted in Moldofsky, "Volleyball," p. 105.
40. Quoted in Dennis G. Steers, "Lang Ping," *Volleyball Monthly,* August 1988, p. 82.
41. Sue Macy, "Golden Moments—The Top 10 Achievements in Women's Olympic History—1984: U.S. Volleyball Goes with the 'Flo,'" WSN. www.wsnsports.com/jsp/ViewEventArticle.jsp?eventId=142&articleId=2802.

42. Quoted in Robert Markel and Nancy Brooks, *For the Record: Women in Sports*. New York: World Almanac, 1985, p. 187.
43. Franz Lidz, "Banker of the Beach," *Sports Illustrated,* June 22, 1992, p. 35.
44. Quoted in Lessa, *Stories of Triumph*, p. 107.
45. Quoted in "Steve Timmons," Volleyball Worldwide. www.volleyball.org/people/steve_timmons.html.

Epilogue: Volleyball Moves into Its Second Century

46. Selinger and Blount-Ackermann, "Introduction."

For Further Reading

George Bulman, *Play the Game: Volleyball.* Mechanicsburg, PA: Stackpole Books, 1996. This book describes basic playing techniques for young volleyball players.

Deborah Crisfield, *Winning Volleyball for Girls.* New York: Facts on File, 1995. Written for female players and their coaches, this book offers advice for getting in shape for the game, drills and playing techniques, and strategies for competitive situations.

Julie Jenson, *Fundamental Volleyball.* Minneapolis, MN: Lerner, 1995. Brief history of the game, along with a description of the basic techniques and plays, with many color photographs.

Karch Kiraly with Byron Shewman, *Beach Volleyball.* Champaign, IL: Human Kinetics, 1999. The three-time Olympic gold medalist describes his techniques for conditioning, drills, and various plays used in the beach game, with photos that illustrate spiking, passing, digging, blocking, and other moves.

———, *Karch Kiraly's Championship Volleyball.* New York: Simon & Schuster, 1990. A world-famous player offers tips on how to play the game.

Christina Lessa, *Stories of Triumph: Women Who Win in Sport and in Life.* New York: Universe, 1998. This beautifully illustrated book contains inspiring profiles of women who have overcome obstacles to succeed.

Lincoln Library of Sports Champions. Columbus: Frontier, 1989. This multivolume set contains profiles of hundreds of top athletes, including volleyball players Mary Jo Peppler and Karcsi (Karch) Kiraly.

Terry Liskevych with Don Patterson, *Youth Volleyball: Championship Skills.* Chicago: NTC, 1995. An Olympic coach describes winning techniques for offensive and defensive play.

Terri Morgan, *Gabrielle Reece: Model Athlete.* Minneapolis: Lerner, 1999. A biography for young people describing the life and achievements of the beach volleyball star who is also a fashion model and TV commentator.

Gabrielle Reece and Karen Karbo, *Big Girl in the Middle.* New York: Crown, 1997.The six feet three Reece describes life as a pro beach volleyball player, as well as a model and television personality, and discusses barriers that women must overcome to succeed in sports.

Works Consulted

Books

Lois Banner, *American Beauty.* New York: Knopf, 1983. A social history that covers the changing ideals of physical beauty for American women, showing the transition from frail and delicate to muscular and athletic.

Steven Boga, *Volleyball.* Mechanicsburg, PA: Stackpole Books, 1997. Along with a brief history of the game, Boga gives readers the rules, strategies, and techniques used in volleyball.

George Gipe, *The Great American Sports Book.* Garden City, NY: Doubleday, 1978. Basic information and colorful anecdotes in this extensive look at numerous sports in American history.

Darlene A. Kluka and Peter J. Dunn, *Volleyball.* Boston: McGraw-Hill, 2000. This book, which briefly describes the origins of the game, discusses the rules and playing techniques for young people.

Robert E. Laveaga, *Volleyball, A Man's Game.* New York: A. S. Barnes, 1933. This classic first book on the game discusses its history, growth, and rules and techniques for playing volleyball.

Jane Leder, *Grace and Glory: A Century of Women in the Olympics.* Washington, D.C.: Multi-media Partners, 1996. Leder shows the history of women's increasing participation in the Olympics in a growing number of events, including a dramatic account of the Japanese women's volleyball team's 1964 triumph.

Robert Markel and Nancy Brooks, *For the Record: Women in Sports.* New York: World Almanac, 1985. Fascinating history of women in various sports, including volleyball, with profiles of top players.

James Naismith, *Basketball: Its Origin and Development.* Lincoln: University of Nebraska Press, 1996. The inventor of this popular game discusses its creation and development in this reprint of a 1941 edition.

Mary Jo Peppler, *Inside Volleyball for Women.* Chicago: Henry Regnery, 1977. A classic instruction manual for women players by Hall of Fame inductee player and coach Mary Jo Peppler.

Arie Selinger with Joan Blount-Ackermann, *Power Volleyball.* New York: St. Martin's, 1986. This book, by the coach who helped the U.S. women win the Olympic silver medal in 1984, describes Selinger's approach to the game and specific strategies for success, shown in more than three hundred photos and diagrams.

Periodicals

J. A. Adande, "Kiraly, Steffes Discover Gold on the Beach," *Washington Post*, July 29, 1996.

Dennis Brown, "Surprise of the Games?" *Volleyball Monthly,* August 1988.

J. Y. Cameron, "The Original Game of Volley Ball," *Physical Education*, July 1896.

Lee Diekemper, "Teammates Hope to Keep Gold Rush," *Tampa Tribune,* April 21, 2001.

Michael Dobie, "The 1996 Atlanta Summer Games/What's New for '96/Beach Volleyball: From Sand to Sand Dollars," *Newsday,* July 14, 1996.

Michael Farber, "Fun in the Sun," *Sports Illustrated,* August 5, 1996.

Bud Greenspan, "My Favorite Olympic Moments," *Sports Illustrated,* June 17, 1996.

Ken Grosse, "Olympics to Showcase International Superstars," *Volleyball Monthly,* August 1988.

Paul Hampel, "Still the Queen of Kills," *St. Louis Post-Dispatch*, July 24, 1997.

Hygeia Magazine, "Women and Sports," November 1928.

Joanne Kabak, "Beach Volleyball/A Cool Sport That's Hot," *Newsday,* July 1, 1996.

Anna de Koven, "The Athletic Woman," *Good Housekeeping,* August 1912.

David Kraft, "The WPVA's Special," *Volleyball Monthly,* March 1992.

Franz Lidz, "Banker of the Beach," *Sports Illustrated,* June 22, 1992.

Vicki Michaelis, "IOC Board to Hear Progress Reports," *USA Today*, December 12, 2000.

Leora Moldofsky, "Volleyball—the Explosive Cubans Don't Just Want to Win; They're Out to Set a Gold-Medal Record," *Time International,* September 18, 2000.

David Leon Moore, "Beach Volleyball Digs Deep to Heal Wounds: Men, Women Eye the Sport's Revival," *USA Today*, April 1, 1999.

Merrell Noden, "A Rare Old Bird," *Sports Illustrated,* May 25, 1992.

Gabrielle Reece, "Learning Curves," *Women's Sports & Fitness*, July 1999.

J. D. Reed, "Beach Volleyball Nets Big Bucks; Once a Laid-Back Pastime, a Waterside Game Goes Major League," *Time*, August 28, 1989.

Glenn Scott, "Big Red," *Volleyball Monthly,* October 1991.

———, "Gold Prices Have Skyrocketed," *Volleyball Monthly*, August 1988.

Sports Illustrated, "Who Needs Water? Just Add Sand," August 5, 1996.

Dennis G. Steers, "Lang Ping," *Volleyball Monthly*, August 1988.

Jon Stevenson, "Flyin' Masakayan Hopes to Soar," *Volleyball Monthly,* February 1988.

———, "Mysteries of the Sand Revealed," *Volleyball Monthly,* June 1988.

Volleyball Monthly, "Cuba Joins North Korea on 'Out' List," February 1988.

Volleyball Monthly, "International Notebook," March 1992.

Volleyball Monthly, "Smith-Stoklos Still Lead Player Parade," February 1992.

Bernie Wilson, "Cuba Wins Volleyball Gold," *Washington Post,* August 3, 1996.

Internet Sources

Association Athletic Handbook—Volleyball 1897, Official Handbook of the Young

Men's Christian Associations of North America online, Volleyball Worldwide. www.volleyball.org/rules/rules_1897.html.

Association of VolleyBall Professionals (AVP), "History." www.avptour.com/tour_history.cfm.

"Athlete's Voice: Sinjin Smith." http://sydney2000.nbcolympics.com/athletesvoice/bv/smithsin/index_smithsin.html.

Joshua W. Binder, "Beach Volleyball." www.brntwdmagazine.com/june01/games/games-1.html.

Mike Bresnahan, "Legendary Player Plans to End His Career at Manhattan," Association of Volleyball Professionals (AVP), August 11, 2001. www.avptour.com/whats_new.cfm?Whats_new_article=6447.

"Child and Heese Plan to Dig in on the Beach for Another Olympic Medal," FIV Volleyball News from Volleyballstuff.com, September 4, 2000. http://cnews.tribune.com/news/story/0,1162,newsday-olympics-72540,00.html.

"Cuba Volleyball." www.cubavball.cjb.net.

Lisa Dillman, "Americans Beat Brazil for Beach Volleyball Gold," *Los Angeles Times* online, September 26, 2000. www.dainblanton.com/olympics2.htm.

"Faculty Profile: Kathy Gregory," UCSB. www.catalog.ucsb.edu/2000cat/profiles/gregory.htm.

"FIVB Mission Statement," www.volleyball.org/fivb/.

"FIVB's 100 Year History of Volleyball," Volleyball Hall of Fame. www.volleyball.org/FIVB.htm.

"Herbert Hoover—Hoover Ball," National Archives and Records Administration, Herbert Hoover Presidential Library and Museum. http://hoover.nara.gov/education/hooverball.html.

"History of the Volleyball Hall of Fame, 1971–1999," Volleyball Hall of Fame. www.volleyhall.org/history.htm.

"History of Volleyball in the Olympics," World Volleyball Association. www.ligavallecaucanavoleibol.com.co/olimpicosvol.htm.

"Inductees and Honorees of the Volleyball Hall of Fame," Volleyball Hall of Fame. www.volleyhall.org/inductees.htm.

"Interview with Nikolai Karpol," *V-Spirit World Volleyball Online Magazine*. www.v-spirit.com/russia/karpol990805int1.html.

"Karch Kiraly," *Volleyball Worldwide*. www.volleyball.org/people/karch_kiraly.html.

"Karolyn Kirby." www.volleyball.org/people/karolyn_kirby.htm.

"Karolyn Kirby's Page." www.spies.com/~islands/jb/vbfiles/kirby.html.

"Kent Steffes." www.volleyball.org/people/kent_steffes.html.

"Kent Steffes, Career Summary." www.bvbdb.com/players/men/kentsteffes.shtml.

"Lang Ping Awarded Best Volleyball Coach in Italy," *People's Daily* Online, November 30, 2000. http://english.peopledaily.com.cn/200011/30/eng20001130_56550.html.

"Liz Masakayan, Pro Beach Volleyball Athlete." www.lmasakayan.com/.

"Lou Henry Hoover." http://hoover.nara.gov/education/louhenrybio.html.

Sue Macy, "Golden Moments—The Top 10 Achievements in Women's Olympic History—1984: U.S. Volleyball Goes with the

'Flo,'" WSN. www.wsnsports.com/jsp/ViewEventArticle.jsp?eventId=142&articleId=2802.

"Rule Changes." www.volleyball.org/rules/index.html.

"Rules of the Game of Volleyball." www.volleyball.org/rules/index.html.

"Sinjin Smith." www.volleyball.org/people/sinjin_smith.html.

"Steve Timmons." www.volleyball.org/people/steve_timmons.html.

"Sunkist Youth Tour," Association of Volleyball Professionals, February 10, 2000. www.avptour.com/whats_new.cfm?Whats_new_article=6193.

Title IX, Education Amendments of 1972 (Title 20 U.S.C. Sections 1681–1688). www.dol.gov/dol/oasam/public/regs/statutes/titleix.htm.

"20th Century Best in Volleyball," FIVB press release, December 11, 2000. www.fivb.ch/Press%20Releases/PR%202000.11.28.html.

"USA Volleyball News," USA Volleyball News Headlines, December 12, 2000. www.usavolleyball.org/news/news_121200.htm.

"Volleyball Athlete Bios." http://sydney2000.nbcolympics.com/bios/.

"Volleyball Chat with Sinjin Smith," About.com, February 24, 1998. http://ad.doubleclick.net/adi/about.com/sports_volleyball;svc=;site=volleyball;kw=;chan=sports;syn=about;pos=vmslot1;sz=120x600;ord=11084475261933991.5.

"Volleyball in the United States of America." www.volleyball.org/usa/index.html.

"Wahine Outlast BYU in Marathon WAC Championship Final; Title Match Longest in NCAA History," *College Sports News Daily* press release, December 1, 1998. http://chili.collegesportsnews.com/scripts/colleges/faxbody.idc?FaxID=24462.

Jason Williams, "Ex-Teammates Win with Others," *Cincinnati Post* Online, June 20, 1998. www.cincypost.com/sports/1998/avp062098.html.

"The WPVA: The Players." http://srd.yahoo.com/goo/Karolyn+Kirby/5/*http://www.sportsline.com/u/wpva/players/athletes/.

Websites

Association of Volleyball Professionals (AVP). www.volleyball.org/avp/.

Fédération Internationale de Volleyball (FIVB). www.volleyball.org/fivb/.

United States Volleyball Association (USVBA). www.volleyball.org/usav/.

USA Volleyball. http://66.113.25.110/.

Volleyball Worldwide. www.volleyball.org/rules/rules_1897.html.

Women's Sports Foundation. www.womenssportsfoundation.org/.

Index

Picture Credits

Cover photo: © Hulton-Deutsch Collection/CORBIS
AP/Wide World, 34, 37, 39, 43, 45, 47, 50, 59, 61, 65, 67, 68, 70, 73,77
© Bettmann/CORBIS, 27
© CORBIS, 19
© Rick Doyle/CORBIS, 56
Hulton/Archive by Getty Images, 18
© Hulton-Deutsch Collection/Corbis, 24
© Kevin Schafer/CORBIS, 9
© Phil Schermeister/CORBIS, 29, 52
© Richard Smith/CORBIS, 8
Volleyball Hall of Fame, 12, 13, 15, 31, 40, 41, 48, 55

About the Author

Victoria Sherrow holds B.S. and M.S. degrees from Ohio State University. Among her writing credits are numerous stories and articles, ten books of fiction, and more than fifty books of nonfiction for children and young adults. Her recent books have explored such topics as biomedical ethics, the Great Depression, and the Holocaust. For Lucent Books, she has written *The Titanic, Life During the Gold Rush,* and *The Righteous Gentiles.* Sherrow lives in Connecticut with her husband, Peter Karoczkai, and their three children.